C000274541

ON SET!

ON SET!

The Insider's Guide to the Secret Locations of Britain's Top TV Series

Steve Clark

BLAKE

Published by Blake Publishing Ltd,
3 Bramber Court, 2 Bramber Road,
London W14 9PB, England

First published in the UK 1999

ISBN 1 85782 3915

All rights reserved. No part of this publication may be
reproduced, stored in a retrieval system, or in any form
or by any means, without the prior permission in writing
of the publisher, nor be otherwise circulated in any form
of binding or cover other than that in which it is published
and without a similar condition including this condition
being imposed on the subsequent purchaser.

British Library Cataloguing-in-Publication Data:
A catalogue record for this book is available
from the British Library.

Designed by GDAdesign

Printed in Great Britain by
Creative Print and Design (Wales), Ebbw Vale, Gwent

1 3 5 7 9 10 8 6 4 2

© Text copyright Steve Clark

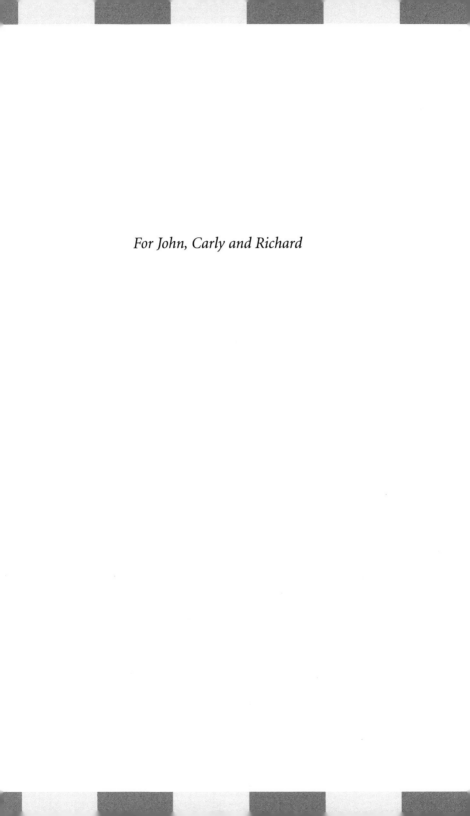

For John, Carly and Richard

CONTENTS

SCOTLAND

THE NORTH

THE NORTH WEST

EAST ANGLIA

THE MIDLANDS

WALES

IRELAND

LONDON

THE HOME COUNTIES

THE SOUTH EAST

THE SOUTH WEST

THE ISLE OF WIGHT

JERSEY

ACKNOWLEDGEMENTS

My thanks go to everyone who has helped with the research for this book, but especially to the following: All the television production and publicity staff who took time out from their busy schedules to help, particularly: Jimmy Perry, Mike Bartley, Russell Lodge, John Booth, Ray Butt, Brian Kaczynski, Alan Ayres, Denise McGurk, Peter Mares, Tracey Whitton, Wendy Dickinson, Richard Haynes and Justine Fouracre; the late Geraint Morris; leading photographer Ken Loveday, who took many of the pictures; Judy Lewthwaite for her help recalling the filming of *The Onedin Line*; Helen Ibbotson for her memories and photographs of *Open All Hours*; Richard Briers for his recollection of filming *The Good Life*, Bill Pertwee for his

Dad's Army memories; Jack Wheeler and John Simpson of the *Dad's Army* Appreciation Society; Gillian French of The Friends of Shipley Windmill and Geraldine Jones of the Historic House Association.

Last, but certainly not least, John Blake, Graeme Andrew, Charly Helyar and Adam Parfitt at Blake Publishing.

INTRODUCTION

There can't be many of us who haven't at some point while watching a television series, asked out loud, or at the very least thought: "I wonder where that was filmed?" Well, hopefully this book will solve many of those puzzles.

It can be enjoyed both by people who do their location spotting simply while sitting at home in front of the box and also the more adventurous who actually want to go one step further and visit some of the places that they've seen on screen.

From the splendour of Castle Howard, the setting for *Brideshead Revisited* to the streets of Bristol where many episodes of *Only Fools and Horses* were filmed, hopefully there's something for everyone.

Television companies go to great lengths to find the perfect locations for their series and the places they choose aren't necessarily famous. Amongst them are some of the best-kept secrets of British countryside and heritage, many well-worth visiting.

Whilst many of the locations and places included in this book are open to the public, there are some that are people's private homes and readers are asked to remember this and respect their privacy.

The maps included are designed to give a clear and simple idea of where some of the places covered in this book can be found. They do not include every local road and are not drawn to scale.

Whilst every effort has been taken to check that all details contained in this book are correct at the time of going to press, readers may wish to confirm opening times before setting out on a long journey.

Happy location hunting.

Steve Clark, 1999

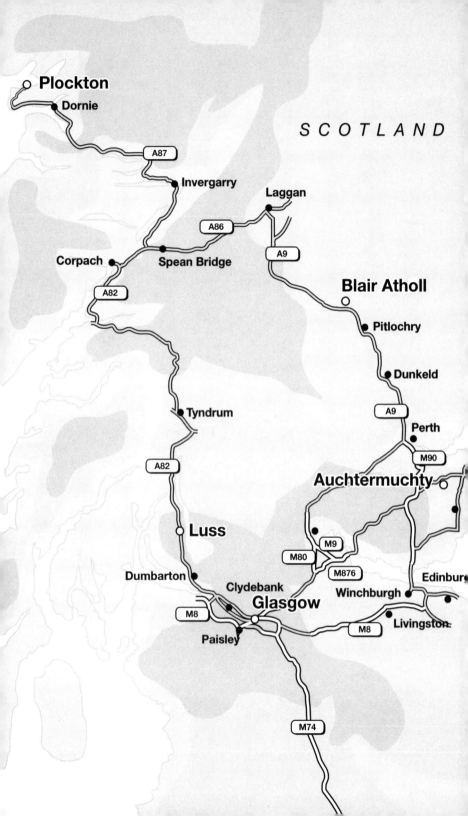

SCOTLAND

HAMISH MACBETH

Plockton, Rosshire

The sleepy village of Plockton on the northwest coast of Scotland found fame as the fictional village of Lochdubh, home beat of PC Hamish Macbeth, played by Robert Carlyle, who has gone on to star in such films as *The Full Monty* and *Trainspotting*.

To find the right location to play Lochdubh for the BBC series, the show's producers toured 1,200 miles of the West Coast of Scotland. 'As soon as we saw Plockton we knew it was perfect,' says Producer Deirdre Keir. 'It's extraordinarily beautiful, it's not on a main road and it has the same kind of close-knit community as Lochdubh.'

Although remote, Plockton is just over the sea from Skye, and it attracts visitors from all over the world. It lies in a sheltered inlet, surrounded by heather-clad mountains and with views across Loch Carron; the Gulf Stream climate accounts for unexpected palm trees which fringe its harbour, and seals are a common sight in its calm waters.

Before the BBC team arrived in the village *en masse* Deirdre and her team made sure the locals were happy with the prospect of a 70-strong film unit arriving. They called a meeting with Charlie McRae, Chairman of the Community Council, and the village elders. 'We spelt out the disadvantages as well as the advantages,' says Deirdre. 'We explained that it would be good for business but that a certain amount of disruption was inevitable. Luckily the villagers voted for the filming to go ahead.'

Plockton's newsagent Edmund McKenzie agreed to move his shop into the sailing club next door for three months so that his premises could be used by the BBC and converted into the Lochdubh general store. Visitors to Plockton were constantly surprised to find the village shop was faked and stocked only with props.

The whitewashed house chosen to be both Hamish's home and the police station is a holiday home owned by a Glasgow doctor. On one occasion a family from London who had pre-booked a week's holiday arrived to find their cottage adorned with a blue lamp and bars at the window and a police cell where a bedroom used to be.

Bed and breakfast business boomed with the influx of cast and crew and the pub extended its mealtimes to fit in with the film schedule. Locals from miles around took part as extras and children from the local school auditioned for small parts. 'We became part of the community,' says Deirdre. 'We had to understand and respect village life in the same way as Hamish Macbeth does. After all, the village could do without us but we couldn't do without our village.'

The production made a contribution towards Plockton's fund-raising project to restore the village hall. 'The village hall was heavily featured in the series,' says Deirdre. 'So it's nice to think that it will benefit directly from our presence.'

Ironically, some of the reasons that made Plockton a perfect choice for the series also caused the production team some headaches. The village is two hours away from the nearest airport and shopping centre, and Glasgow, where many of the cast and crew lived, is a five-hour drive away in good weather. Many of the roads in the area are single-track and more suited to sheep than large film trucks and buses. Not being on a main road, Plockton gets little conventional traffic, so a herd of highland cattle has right of way through the village and cows frequently held up filming as they ambled along. Mobile phones and walkie-talkies, essential to modern film units, didn't work in Plockton and that lack of easy communication was a constant problem. 'When we arrived the villagers thought we were mad, living our lives at such breakneck speed,' says Deirdre. 'After a while we realised that they were right. Things went a lot smoother when we adjusted to local time.'

HIGH ROAD

Luss, Strathclyde

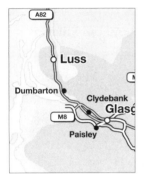

The Scottish soap is filmed at Luss on the bank of Loch Lomond where the pretty village doubles as fictional Glendarroch.

The big house in the series is actually the Youth Hostel at nearby Arden, which can be seen from the main road, and the Hostel's annexe nearby plays the Glendarroch Hotel in the series, although the interior shots are recorded in the studio. Anyone wanting to stay at the hostel must be a member of the Youth Hostel Association.

In Luss itself, filming takes place at the Highland Arts Gift Shop – which plays Blair's Store – outside several cottages, at the church and at the manse. The ferry used to feature regularly and we still see characters walking along the beach and on the pier. A farm at nearby Glenfruin is also featured.

The nearby town of Helensburgh also appears in the series for lots of shop scenes and the Coffee Club in Colquhoun Square appears regularly.

DOCTOR FINLAY

Auchtermuchty, Fife

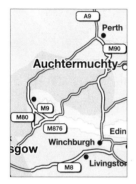

Auchtermuchty became the fictional Scottish town of Tannochbrae in the 1993 series of *Doctor Finlay* by chance when the series' producer Peter Wolfes drove through the town on his way to view another possible location. The industrial and farming town, which is in north east Fife, fitted the bill perfectly because it had a by-pass round it which meant that there was not too much traffic to disrupt filming. In addition, the centre point of the town, The Cross, is a conservation area so the buildings needed little alteration to fit the period of the programme.

'Traffic is always the biggest downfall for filming,' says Brian Kaczynski, Location Manager on *Doctor Finlay*. 'Because of either the noise or having to divert the traffic.' Even though Auchtermuchty was well suited to play Tannochbrae, the series production team still had to spend a lot of time turning the clock back to the 1950s before filming began. As Brian says: 'To actually find a town frozen in time would be impossible.' So, shop fronts and signs were altered, modern road markings covered up and streetlights changed. Many buildings in The Cross were used for filming and The Forest Hills Hotel became a temperance hotel, The Salvation. The post office appeared regularly in the first series – although viewers are unlikely to have recognised it. Scottish Television, which made *Doctor Finlay*, turned it into The Flying Dutchman pub by covering the real exterior with false walls.

The church that appeared on screen was really two – the outside shots were filmed at Auchtermuchty Church but the interior shots took place at Old Monklands Parish Church, in the middle of a sprawling council estate at Cokebridge, just east of Glasgow. Brian Kaczynski explained: 'The church at Auchtermuchty is lovely, but the colouring of the wood is so light that it would have been too bright on film.'

Auchtermuchty Town Hall, which was the town's police station many years ago and still has the old cells, reverted back to its former role to play Tannochbrae Police Station. The town's council offices doubled as the local bank and the entrance to the library was altered to fit the 1950s and was used as Tannochbrae Library.

The STV team had nothing but praise for the people of Auchtermuchty who had to put up with the occasional closure of roads and restricted parking during filming. Said Brian: 'It was all credit to them because most of them weren't helped directly by the filming, so we relied on their goodwill and they were exceptionally good about it.' Many of the local people were used as extras in the series.

What was missing from Auchtermuchty, of course, was the surgery, Arden House, and that was because it wasn't in the town. In fact, it was more than 70 miles away on a country estate just outside Glasgow. Said Brian: 'The doctor's car would drive down the street and then reappear at the surgery – and they would have gone 71 miles.' Arden House was actually an old farmhouse and was chosen because of its proximity to STV's studios. Designers built a road up to the house over the top of the old farm track, built a false street of houses opposite and brought in old-fashioned streetlights.

The house is on a private estate and so it cannot be visited, which was a blessing for the production team because there was no noise from traffic to interrupt filming. Most of the picturesque scenes for *Doctor Finlay* were shot at Loch Lomond or further north in the Trossachs. Said Brian: 'That's where we did many of the picnic, river and driving shots.'

The original sixties series *Doctor Finlay's Casebook* was filmed in Callander but STV producers decided not to use it for the 1993 series because it had become too busy. 'Callander has changed quite dramatically over the last 20 years and is now very busy as it's on the main tourist route to the north,' explained Brian. 'It was probably controllable in the sixties but now you would cause pandemonium if you tried to close it for the amount of time we require. Callander is a lovely place but it just wasn't practical.'

STRATHBLAIR

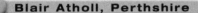

Blair Atholl, Perthshire

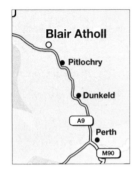

Finding an ideal farm to double as windswept Corriebeg in the BBC drama *Strathblair* was easy – thanks to the series' agricultural adviser Ben Coutts. Ben used to be a hill farmer not far from the Perthshire village where *Strathblair* is filmed – and remembered an old, empty farm.

Luckily for the BBC the farmhouse was still empty and, although the barns were full of hay and the land was still used for sheep, the owner agreed to rent it out. In the drama, when newlyweds Alec and Jennifer Ritchie arrive at Corriebeg, they find it in a poor state – and in real life the farm fitted that bill. But the BBC still had to make it look more run down. 'We aged the timber with a lot of paint treatment and put in older guttering and down pipes so that it really looked sad,' says Production Designer Alex Gourlay.

Scenes for the first series inside the Corriebeg farmhouse were recorded on sets built at BBC studios. But for the second series, Alex and his team cleared out the inside of the farmhouse, including removing the old floor, and the interior shots were actually filmed inside the real farmhouse – ideal for days when outside shooting was interrupted by rain or snow.

The design team built a dutch barn because the script required one and added a hen house bought from a local farmer. They also scoured the local countryside for authentic farm props and filled the farm with broken bits of machinery.

Strathblair village was the biggest location on the series. 'We looked around for a suitable village with the least amount of anachronisms for 1950,' says Alex. They settled on the village of Blair Atholl in Perthshire, but if you visit it you won't be able to find some of the shops you saw on screen. That's because Alex and his team built the grocer's shop, which served two purposes: it was needed in the script, and it covered up some modern buildings. The shop, which was kitted out with 1950s packets and jars hired and copied from museums and collections, also sprouted two fake cottages next door which were so authentic they fooled visitors to the village during filming.

'By building a fake street they could shoot 360 degrees,' explains Alex, who also built the front of a butcher's shop, which concealed the brightly-coloured local Spar shop. The fictional Laird's house is in a neighbouring village and in real life is private and belongs to a retired army officer. 'We only use the outside and we have a complete interior set in the studio so all we have to do there is to make sure the drapes and blinds match the ones we have in the studio,' says Alex.

TAGGART

Glasgow

Maryhill Police Station, home to Detective Inspector Mike Jardine, played by James Macpherson, and his sidekick Detective Sergeant Jackie Reid, played by Blythe Duff, in the Scottish Television detective series *Taggart*, has had a facelift or two over the years. The exterior of Partick Police Station in Glasgow used to double as Maryhill but the police have now moved to a new site and the old location has become a drug rehabilitation centre so it is now rarely used.

Scenes are now usually filmed at night at Turnball Street Police Station, which is used by the police as a holding centre for prisoners brought from prisons before they go to court. The station isn't used at night so the *Taggart* team is allowed to film in the cells too, and the rest of the interior of the police station is filmed at a former finance office in a Glasgow shipyard.

Mortuary scenes for *Taggart* used to be filmed at the real police mortuary next to the High Court in Glasgow, but it wasn't easy. 'It became too difficult because we'd have to pull out if there was a murder or a body found and they had to do a quick post-mortem,' explains *Taggart* Location Manager John Booth.

The *Taggart* production team then tried several

hospital mortuaries, but have now settled on the freezing room at the Glasgow College of Food Technology in Cathedral Street, where students going into the catering industry are taught how to freeze food. 'They've got a big room with freezers and white tiled walls, although the trouble with the freezers is they are not deep enough so we have to film half a body at a time and shoot it at the right angle.'

Two bars used regularly for *Taggart* are the Halt Bar in Woodlands Road and the Scotia Bar in Stockwell Street, although they usually look different in each *Taggart* story because different directors shoot from different angles.

The police give the *Taggart* team full co-operation when it comes to filming. 'The police are brilliant,' says John Booth. 'And they do their best to accommodate us if we need to close a street.'

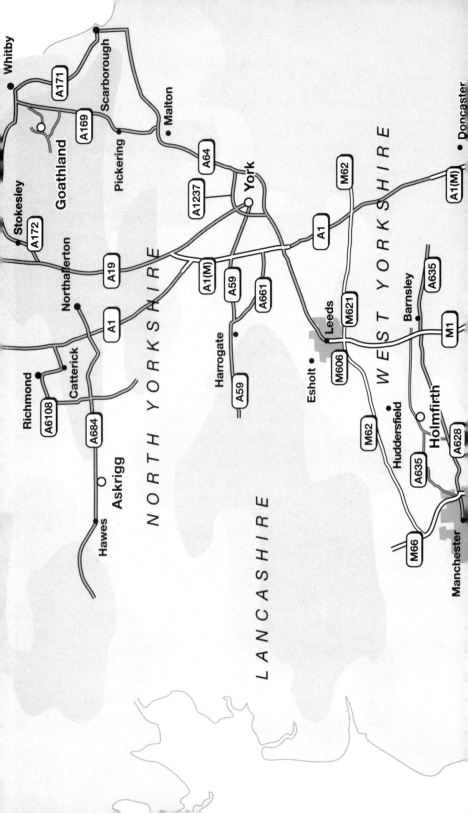

THE NORTH

LAST OF THE SUMMER WINE

The gentle comedy *Last of the Summer Wine* has given the Yorkshire town of Holmfirth the sort of publicity that tourist industry chiefs can usually only dream of. Since it began more than 20 years ago, the series has put the town firmly on the tourist map and shown off the full beauty of the Pennine countryside.

Each year, thousands of fans flock to Holmfirth to see for themselves the real-life haunts of three of television's most lovable old eccentrics Compo, Foggy and Clegg, played by Bill Owen, Brian Wilde and Peter Sallis.

First port of call in Holmfirth – particularly after a long drive – must be to the café used as Sid's Café in the series. A former paint store for a nearby hardware shop, the cafe now looks much the same off-screen as on, and the BBC,

who have always used the outside for filming, now sometimes use the inside as well. When current owner Colin Frost took the cafe on he says he looked on it as a challenge. 'And it has been a challenge all right,' he says. 'It's hard work but we've made a success out of it.' One of Colin's bright ideas, which have been part of the café's

success story, was to sell a range of Sid's Café merchandise, and the list is now booming with items for sale ranging from Ivy's slippers to mugs and plates to children's colouring kits.

'I've turned the café round from a straight café to a tourist attraction,' says Colin. 'And we have people in from all round the world including New Zealand and Canada – most countries seem to get the series now on satellite.'

Colin has nothing but praise for the impact the success of *Last of the Summer Wine* has had on the town. 'It's done a lot of good for Holmfirth,' he says. 'It has brought it to life.' Colin now

Left: Compo tries a new kind of driving!
PICTURE © KEN LOVEDAY

also runs mini-bus tours of *Last of the Summer Wine* locations both in and out of the town. For details telephone: (01484) 689610.

No trip to Holmfirth is complete without taking a peek at Nora Batty's famous house. It is just a short walk from the café along Hollowgate. At the end of Hollowgate is a bridge and from it you can see Nora's house, number 28 Scarfold, and below is the door to Compo's flat. But don't expect to see Nora because in real life it is a private house, so you'll have to be content with a visit to the Wrinkled Stocking tea-room next door. Underneath Nora's steps is the flat that plays Compo's home in the series, and it now houses a *Last of the Summer Wine* Exhibition. Both the tea-room and the exhibition are open seven days a week all year round, but off-season it's best to check exact opening times by telephoning: (01484) 681408.

You might also enjoy visiting the Holmfirth Postcard Museum in Huddersfield Road. You may also like to call in for a pint at Compo, Foggy and Clegg's local, The White Horse Inn at Jackson Bridge. To find it, leave Holmfirth on the A635 to Barnsley. Travel to New Mill then bear right onto the A616 Sheffield Road and then after about ¾ of a mile turn right towards Jackson Bridge and Hepworth and you'll then enter Jackson Bridge and see the pub on your right. From Jackson Bridge you may like to drive to Hepworth where you'll find another of the trio's locals, The Butcher's Arms.

ALL CREATURES GREAT AND SMALL

Askrigg, North Yorkshire

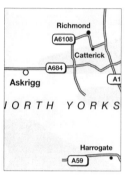

All Creatures Great and Small was based on the semi-autobiographical novels of vet James Herriot, and the series starred Christopher Timothy as Herriot, Robert Hardy as his partner Siegfried Farnon and Peter Davison as Tristan Farnon.

The real-life surgery on which the James Herriot books are based is in Thirsk, but the BBC plumped for the picturesque village of Askrigg to play fictional Darrowby. Thirsk was rejected because it looked too modern, whereas Askrigg remains unspoilt and can play a thirties or forties village with ease.

On arrival in Askrigg you'll notice the market cross, and on the right is tall Skeldale House which played the vets' surgery. We never actually saw the characters go through the door into the house; instead we saw them approach the door and the action then followed on a set of the interior built in a BBC studio. The house, notable for its railings, is now an Abbeyfield home for the elderly, but it looks just the same as it did in the series.

Next door is a newsagent's shop, which played a sweet shop in the series, and across the road from it is the real-life grocer's shop which played the same in the series. The shop needed very little set dressing by the BBC to take the role, and still looks almost identical to the way we saw it on screen.

A few yards up the hill from the grocer's shop is The King's Arms Hotel, which played The Drover's Arms. The hotel's back parlour also appeared in the series for interior shots and was the place where Tristan and James were seen downing many a pint with locals. The bar fitted the bill perfectly for the production as it still has original saddle hooks in the ceiling. These were used by the BBC to hang up their lighting equipment. The hotel was built for John Pratt in 1760 to house his then-famous racing stables, and was converted to a coaching inn in 1810. Today the hotel retains its traditional character and charm combined with modern day comfort. Further details: (01969) 650258.

Not far from Askrigg is Bolton Castle, which has been owned by the same family for 600 years, and which was used in the series as the place where James proposed to Helen. It has an interesting history: Mary Queen of Scots was kept there for several months during the 16th century and it was defended by the Royalists during the English Civil War. It has recently been used again on television as Prince John's castle in the BBC series *Ivanhoe* and the feature film *Elizabeth*. It's open to the public and can also be used for civil wedding ceremonies. Further details can be obtained by calling: (01969) 623981. You can also access its website at http://www.boltoncastle.co.uk

Other locations used in the series include: the market in Hawes, which played Darrowby Cattle Market, Hardraw Church which was Darrowby Church, and Wensley Church where James and Helen were married.

Below: A star line-up for
All Creatures Great and Small.

BRIDESHEAD REVISITED

Castle Howard, near York, Yorkshire

The worldwide success of the ITV epic drama *Brideshead Revisited* has brought thousands of extra visitors flocking to the series' principal location, Castle Howard in Yorkshire. And even now, more than a decade after the series was shown in Britain, it still contributes heavily to the number of visitors to Castle Howard, which has been the seat of the Howard family for more than three centuries. In fact, around a third of people questioned in a recent survey said they came because they had seen the stately home on *Brideshead Revisited*. In addition to British visitors, the programme has been sold to dozens of countries all round the world and helps to attract a steady stream of people from places as far afield as Australia and Zimbabwe.

Brideshead Revisited is often cited as one of ITV's biggest successes – both critically and in terms of ratings – but filming didn't run smoothly. It cost Granada, who made it, more than twice the original budget, a strike by television workers held up production and the crew was disbanded at one point.

When the series finally went into production Granada managed to find a distinguished cast including Laurence

Olivier, John Gielgud, Anthony Andrews and Jeremy Irons.

The tale of love and passion during the inter-war years was filmed against a backdrop of 18th century Castle Howard, one of the finest stately homes in Britain, which is set in 1,000 acres of parkland, and which is as stunning on the outside as it is beautiful inside. For fans of the show, the Garden Hall will bring back memories, for it was the room where Charles Ryder (Jeremy Irons) spent much time painting the panels on the wall. In reality the panels, which depict imaginary follies, were painted by artist Felix Kelly, and replaced those destroyed by a fire in 1940. The famous hunting scene was filmed on Castle Howard's north front, and other major scenes were filmed in the Great Hall, the Music Room and Lady Georgina's bedroom.

Brideshead Revisited is not the only programme to have been filmed at Castle Howard. In 1965 it featured in *Lady L* which starred David Niven, Sophia Loren and Paul Newman; it played the Kremlin in the 1966 film *The Spy With A Cold Nose*; it appeared in Stanley Kubrick's film *Barry Lyndon* in 1975; a BBC version of *Twelfth Night* in 1978; and in 1994 the BBC returned to film the costume drama *The Buccaneers*.

Castle Howard house is open from mid March until late October from 11am, with last admissions at 4.30pm. The grounds and gardens are open all year round from 10am. For further details telephone: (01653) 648333 or look at Castle Howard's web pages at http://www.castlehoward.co.uk

EMMERDALE

Esholt, Yorkshire

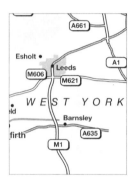

There's good news and bad news for fans of the ITV soap *Emmerdale*. First the good news: you can visit both of the villages used as Beckindale in the series and now go on a tour at the Yorkshire Television studios in Leeds and see the interior sets. The bad news is that you can no longer visit the exterior locations for the show since filming was switched from the village of Esholt to a specially built set on an estate in north Yorkshire in January 1998.

The pretty village of Arncliffe played the first Beckindale, but production was moved in 1976 because the producers decided to find somewhere closer to Leeds, where the interior scenes are recorded, as it was quite a trek to Arncliffe. Not only that, Arncliffe had become such a mecca for fans that the village just couldn't cope. Filming was switched to Esholt, which is just a few miles northwest of Leeds, and that became a magnet for lovers of the show, so much so that a special parking site for coaches had to be built nearby.

In 1997 Yorkshire Television decided to build a purpose - built set elsewhere. The success of the series and the pressures of extra episodes made shooting at Esholt too difficult. It had been fine when they only made one episode a week, but three episodes trebled the workload. The new set, which took four months to build, isn't an exact replica and Yorkshire Television received quite a few letters when it was first seen on-screen because some viewers noticed the change, despite the efforts of expert painters and set constructors.

Even though fans can't now see the new *Emmerdale* set, they can visit the studios where all the interior scenes are filmed including The Woolpack, The Dingle's home and Home Farm. They were opened to the public in January 1997 by former Prime Minister John Major and are open every weekend. For details telephone: (0113) 222 7990.

Esholt is still worth a visit though. As you drive into the village you'll pass the coach park on the left. If you take the next left you'll find yourselves in Main Street and halfway down on the left is The Woolpack pub, with a car park behind. The Woolpack, which used to be called The Commercial until the name was changed to fit in with the show and attract tourists, was only ever used in the series for exterior shots. A few yards down Main Street, also on the left, is the village hall, which has featured extensively in the series.

Just opposite the hall is St Paul's Church which played Beckindale Church, where Matt married Dolly, Kathy married Jackie, and Joe married twice in the series! Out the other side of the church is The Vicarage, which was home for many years to Reverend Donald Hinton, but which in real life has now been turned into three homes.

As you walk down Church Lane you'll see the Ashwood

Tea Rooms, which have been used in the series. The Tea Rooms sell a range of *Emmerdale* memorabilia, from T-shirts to pens – and tea, of course.

Turning left at the end of Church Lane, follow Chapel Lane for a short while until you find Cunliffe Lane. Turn into it and you'll see Bunker's Hill, which was better known on-screen as Demdyke, until it was 'destroyed' in the 1993 plane crash storyline. On-screen, number six played Seth Armstrong's house and number three used to house Nick, Elsa and Alice. And – just a reminder – the houses are homes to real people not connected with *Emmerdale*.

Some of the other scenes in *Emmerdale* are filmed in the nearby town of Otley, which plays Hotten in the series, and Otley Market doubles as Hotten Market.

Below: The Woolpack from *Emmerdale*, formerly The Commercial.

PICTURE © KEN LOVEDAY

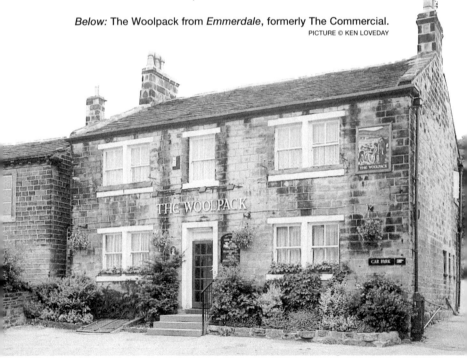

HEARTBEAT

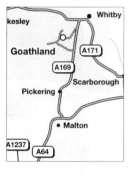

The picturesque North Yorkshire village of Goathland has always been a popular place for tourists due to its superb views of the moors. And using the village as the setting for Yorkshire Television's hit drama *Heartbeat* was guaranteed to bring a host of new visitors. At the start of the series, former *EastEnders* actor Nick Berry played London police constable Nick Rowan who quit his inner-city beat to take a job as a rural village bobby, along with his doctor wife Kate, played by Niamh Cusack.

The series, which is set in the sixties, followed Nick and Kate from the moment they moved into Aidensfield police house. Inevitably, over the eight years the series has now been running, members of the cast have changed. Kate died when Niamh Cusack left and Nick Rowan married schoolteacher Jo Weston, played by Juliette Gruber. Later, Nick Berry left the show with the story seeing Nick Rowan moving to Canada.

PC Phil Bellamy, played by Mark Jordan, continued, and Mike Bradley, played by Jason Durr, moved into Aidensfield. Nurse Maggie Bolton (Kazia Pelka) arrived and was later followed by her doctor husband Neil, played by David Michaels, but he was killed in the spring of 1999 while rescuing a child from a fire. One thing has always stayed the

Nick and Kate enjoy the
Yorkshire countryside.

Inset: The police house where
the couple lived in the series.
PICTURE © KEN LOVEDAY

same – dodgy farmer Claude Greengrass, played by Bill Maynard, continues to wheel and deal, usually unsuccessfully. His old foil, Sergeant Blaketon, has retired and now runs the village post office – but still keeps his eye on Greengrass.

The police station is now run by Sergeant Raymond Craddock, played by Philip Franks, and aided by the two younger PCs and stalwart PC Alf Ventress, played by William Simons. The pub is run by Gina Ward, played by Tricia Penrose, and helped by her Auntie Mary (Arbel Jones).

There's plenty to see in Goathland for *Heartbeat* fans. When you drive through the village you'll reach a right-hand bend and the stone house on your right is Glendale House, which played Kate Rowan's surgery in the series. The house was built in 1875 by Edward Fuller Sewell, an uncle of Anna Sewell, author of the novel *Black Beauty*. It's a Victorian stone-built residence and occupies a prime position in the centre of the picturesque village, overlooking the common, where sheep graze right outside the garden gate. Its owners, Keith and Sandra Simmonds, offer reasonably priced bed and breakfast. For details telephone: (01947) 896281 or see their web page at http://www.falcon internet. co.uk/heartbeat/index.html

Sandra says the impact of *Heartbeat* on Goathland has been positive. '*Heartbeat* has been very good for business and the production team have bent over backwards to minimise disruption to the village,' she says.

Over at Brow House Farm, used as the location for Claude Greengrass' farm, farmers John and Keith Jackson find that honesty pays better and make a nice little earner from their connection with the show by opening up some of their fields as a campsite. 'We had the site up and running before *Heartbeat* began but now people know the series is filmed here they are keener than ever to come and stay,' says Keith. 'We get a lot more people here now because of *Heartbeat*.' In fact, business has been so good recently that the Jacksons have given another field over to campers to cope with demand. 'Business has picked up a lot,' he says, 'and so we opened the other field up because we couldn't get them all on the original site. It seems the more popular *Heartbeat* gets, the busier we are – there's no doubt about that.'

Facilities offered to campers and caravanners include running water, a shower and toilets, and electricity hook-up points. Charges start at around £6.50 a unit per night for caravans and tents or even less for single travellers. Trippers can try their luck at getting a pitch, but it's advisable to book. Bookings can be made by writing to: Brow House Farm, Goathland, North Yorkshire.

The Jacksons also help supplement their income from farming with the modest fees Yorkshire Television pays them for using their farm as a film location – and plough most of it back into the business.

The Jacksons have also become friendly with actor Bill Maynard, who plays layabout Greengrass. 'Bill is brilliant,' says Keith. 'He always has a good natter and always wants to look around. He's just like an everyday farmer when he's here, and he joins in playing pool and darts with us at the pub.'

Real-life Goathland Garage appears in the series as Mostyn's Garage, and across the road from it is The

Goathland Hotel which plays the local pub, The Aidensfield Arms. You'll also see the real post office which plays Oscar Blaketon's post office in the show. A private house, Brereton Cottage, on Brereton Corner played Dr Bolton's surgery.

The Goathland Primary School featured heavily in the show when Nick's wife Jo Weston was in the series, and in real life the school benefited from a donation from Yorkshire Television which helped kit the pupils out in new school uniforms.

What was always missing from Goathland was the police house. And that's because it isn't in Goathland at all. In fact, it's around 70 miles away, near Leeds. To find it, take the A65 from Leeds through Horsforth and Guisley following the signs to Ilkley until you see a sign to Denton and Askwith. Follow the road, which will cross an iron bridge. At the next T-junction turn right towards Denton and Askwith. In Askwith you'll see the Black Horse pub and immediately opposite is the house which plays the police house. And by the magic of television (and clever editing) it always looks as if it's up on the moors in Goathland. And – just a reminder – the house is private.

To find the police station, where grumpy Sergeant Craddock works, leave Askwith without going back the way you've just come, and head towards Otley. Follow the road until you arrive in Otley and cross the bridge. Then take the second road on the left and at the next T-junction turn right and then take the next right into Courthouse Street. The building used in *Heartbeat* as the police station, which really was a police station, is then on the right.

OPEN ALL HOURS

15 Lister Avenue, Doncaster, South Yorkshire

You won't find Arkwright's grocery open all hours if you go to number 15 Lister Avenue in Doncaster. Nor will you be able to buy a p-p-p-packet of cornflakes or a l-l-l-loaf of bread. But you might be able to get your hair cut! The shop that played stuttering Arkwright's shop in the highly successful BBC comedy *Open All Hours*, and became Britain's best-known shop front, is actually a hair salon.

The BBC picked the shop because it had a traditional double front and fitted the bill perfectly as Arkwright's old-style corner shop. So for three weeks a year, four years running, the BBC rolled their camera equipment into the street and moved owner Helen Ibbotson's hairdryers and curlers out of her shop. They covered up Helen's 'Beautique' sign with a board bearing Arkwright's name, and dressed up the front of the shop with stocks of food. And, of course, they painted details of Arkwright's bargain of the week on the window.

'It was never a real inconvenience,' Helen explains. 'I used to shut down when they were here. The BBC used to pay me very nicely – a bit more than the hairdressing. So it paid for a holiday, which was very handy.'

And Helen got another bonus too – free vegetables! After filming had ended the BBC often used to give her Arkwright's vegetables. 'They gave me a lot of the stuff and I made wine with the parsnips and carrots,' she says.

Helen has good memories of the show's two stars: Ronnie Barker, who played stuttering Arkwright, and David Jason, who played Granville. She says: 'David was a very funny man and nice to get on with. Ronnie was very nice too but a bit more serious than David – but still very jolly. People seemed to like them in the street. They always used to get a good crowd when they were filming.'

And the shop, which used to be a real grocery before Helen took it over, still attracts fans from far afield. 'Fans who are over here from Australia always come to the shop,' says Helen. 'A lady came recently and took some photographs outside the shop and I've become pen pals with a couple of people from Australia who came to see the shop – one of them is an airline pilot.'

Across the road from Helen's shop is number 34 which played the home of Arkwright's love, nurse Gladys Emmanuel (Lynda Baron). After it was used for the first series the then owner of the house altered the look of the front of it, and when the BBC came to make the next series they decided it no longer suited them. So filming was switched to number 32 next door – and the BBC hoped no one would notice.

David Jason and Ronnie Barker share a joke filming *Open All Hours*.

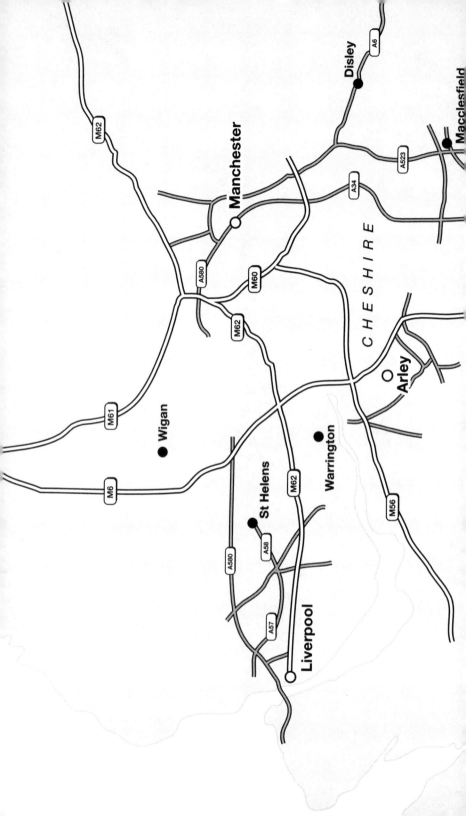

THE NORTH WEST

THE ADVENTURES OF SHERLOCK HOLMES

Manchester

The Baker Street set, which forms part of Granada Studios, Water Lane, Manchester, has been used for the filming of more than two dozen *Sherlock Holmes* adventures since 1984, starring the late Jeremy Brett as Sir Arthur Conan Doyle's detective.

The Arthur Conan Doyle Society worked alongside a Granada Studios team to set up Sherlock's Museum of Criminology, and it is thought to be the biggest collection of Sherlock Holmes-related memorabilia in the country.

During a trip to the set you can step on the famous cobbles and follow in Sherlock Holmes' footsteps, visit his housekeeper Mrs Hudson in the study of number 221b, and buy a range of souvenirs including deerstalkers, pipes, books and videos. For more details telephone Granada Studio Tours on (0161) 833 0880.

The headquarters of Abbey National plc now stands on the site of the fictional home of Sherlock Holmes, 221b Baker Street, London, and the company has marked the significance of the site with a bronze plaque, which was unveiled by Jeremy Brett in 1985. As many as 200 letters a week still arrive at Abbey National addressed to Sherlock Holmes, 221b Baker Street. They are from admirers all over the world wanting to express their admiration or simply enquiring about his wellbeing. Some request his services to find stolen jewels or missing pets. Others ask him to investigate matters of political intrigue. One letter even asked Holmes for advice on how to commit the perfect murder and another person wrote to ask how he could set up a detective agency. Abbey National has a full-time member of staff to deal with the letters and every correspondent receives a reply from Holmes' secretary.

Right: Sherlock Holmes and Dr Watson study a clue.

CLUEDO

Arley Hall, Arley, Cheshire

There is a stately home in Cheshire that has been the scene of more than two dozen murders in the past few years. But it is not quite as grisly as it sounds. For Arley Hall, which is about 18 miles from Manchester, starred as Arlington Grange in ITV's murder mystery gameshow *Cluedo*.

The Hall, which was built between 1832 and 1845, was picked to play The Grange because it has a near perfect layout of downstairs rooms that the game of Cluedo requires. And it wasn't too far from the Manchester studios of Granada, which makes the series, and it is only open to the public at certain times of the year making filming easier.

'The floorplan lent itself to the boardgame very well,' explained Producer Mark Gorton. 'And that was a major consideration when choosing the location. The only room it lacked was a billiard room so we had to construct one.'

The billiard room was created in a front drawing room and, in addition to the billiard table itself, props experts added scoring devices and cues to fit the 1930s period of the show. The library needed little attention to appear on screen, but the dining room had to have a huge table added and a series of gothic high-backed chairs. 'We also added a variety of strange stuffed animals to lend it a kind of *Addams Family* feel,' said Mark.

The drawing room fitted the bill perfectly because of its unusual gothic fireplaces, enhanced by the addition of two leaping gargoyles at either side. The props team also added a suite of high-backed furniture with lion's paw feet, but Mark Gorton says most of the original furniture was ideal for the programme. 'There was a lot of stuff there, like the oil paintings hanging on the walls and various pieces of furniture, that we loved and we kept in the room. As far as the owners were concerned, as long as the items weren't too valuable, we were free to use them.'

Arley Hall, and its beautiful gardens which date back to 1744 and are among the finest in Britain, is privately owned and has become a major tourist attraction since it was opened to the public in 1962. They were more recently used for the filming of Jane Asher's *Good Living* daytime TV series and an episode of the ITV drama *Liverpool One*, and are open from Easter to October. For further details telephone (01565) 777353.

CORONATION STREET

Manchester

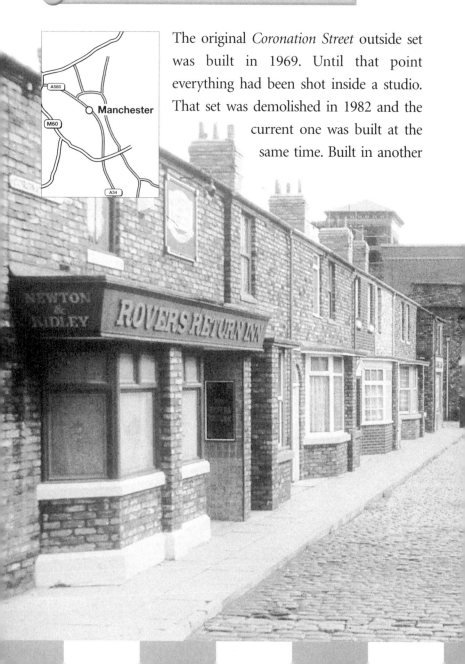

The original *Coronation Street* outside set was built in 1969. Until that point everything had been shot inside a studio. That set was demolished in 1982 and the current one was built at the same time. Built in another part of the Granada Studios, the new set gave the actors and production staff more room in which to work.

Eagle-eyed viewers would have noticed a few changes during the switch – an alley was added between the Rover's Return and Number One Coronation Street, the front of the community centre was updated and the Graffiti Club was built.

Unlike viewers of other soaps, *Coronation Street* fans are fortunate in that they can go and see the real life setting of their favourite show on a tour of the studios. Granada Studios was opened up to the

Left: The world-famous Coronation Street.

Inset: The Sherlock Holmes Granada Studios Tour.

public in July 1988 and since then nearly five million visitors have walked down the famous cobbles of *Coronation Street*. And while visitors are unlikely to see any of the show's stars, they can stand at the bar in the Rover's Return, look through the windows of the Malletts' stone-clad home and peek into Rita's shop. One place you won't see on the tour is Bettabuys, as scenes for that are shot at the Morrisons supermarket at Eccles, when the store is closed to customers.

There's also far more to the award-winning Granada Studios than just the Street. Visitors can step back in time on the Baker Street set, used for Granada TV's *Adventures of Sherlock Holmes*, and take part in a debate at the House of Commons set used in a string of TV productions including *House of Cards*, *To Play The King*, *The New Statesman* and *The Politician's Wife*. Then there's the Backstage Tour which is a fascinating behind-the-scenes look at television, including the chance to read the news, see a control room and editing suite, and learn some of the make-up

Right: Ken Barlow and Mike Baldwin grapple in the Rovers.

artist's tricks of the trade. There are also sets from *Blind Date*, *Emmerdale* and *This Morning*.

For those looking for a little more excitement there are *Robocop* and *Aliens* rides, a UFO Zone and a special effects show. The park is open all year round, but it's best to check before travelling for exact dates and times. For more details telephone Granada Studios on (0161) 833 0880.

BREAD

Elswick Street, Dingle, Liverpool

Liverpool

Elswick Street used to be just another smart row of two-up, two-down terraced houses just a few yards from the river Mersey in Liverpool. But all that changed when a BBC film crew arrived – and it ended up becoming one of the most famous streets in Britain. As the setting for the comedy series *Bread*, Elswick Street became a popular place for tourists to visit. The big Boswell family lived at number 30 on-screen and grumpy Granddad lived next door at number 28.

Bread's writer Carla Lane chose Elswick Street because it fitted the image she had of where the Boswells lived and, as the road ran down to the river Mersey, it suited the scenes she planned to write. 'It was just the right street because I knew I could get some lovely shots of the river running at the bottom of the road and I just thought it was an interesting place,' Carla explains. 'Any street would have been all right, but with the river there I could have Granddad reminiscing about when he was a kid and how the ships came in and it just gave an extra dimension to it all.'

When she writes a script, Carla actually tells the location manager on the show where she thinks something should be filmed. 'I go out on my own and look at places and then I write them into a script. 'And then the BBC go out and find them from there. I give them more than a hint,' she laughs. 'I tell them where!'

The people of Elswick Street didn't seem to mind the interruption that filming brought to their lives. 'They seemed to love it,' Carla recalls. 'They used to come to London to watch the show being recorded in the studio, and we had a big party when the series ended. The people whose houses were used on-screen became very famous because people would come from all over the place just to look at them.'

BROOKSIDE

Liverpool

In the world of television soaps a great deal of time is spent making sets look just like the real thing. Coronation Street, although it looks just like a typical Manchester Street, isn't real and the houses in Albert Square, home of *EastEnders*, don't have backs to them.

Brookside is different. The houses seen on-screen in the Merseyside soap are very real and are in a cul-de-sac on a real estate in the West Derby area of Liverpool. The houses were bought for the programme more than ten years ago by *Brookside* creator Phil Redmond and are separated from real homes nearby by a security barrier. The television location does not welcome visitors and round-the-clock security guards make sure no one can sneak in.

When characters go through an alleyway from Brookside Close and arrive at Brookside Parade shops it looks as if they've just walked a few yards. But that is just a clever illusion of television. For in actual fact the Brookside Parade, offices and the petrol station scenes are filmed five miles away on the site of a former further education college at Childwall. Scenes of characters arriving at the Parade from the Close look as if they take seconds – but they are often filmed days apart.

The actual college building is also used for the programme, and saves the production team having to find new locations outside. It's a flexible building and has played a school, a police station and a hospital. A high wall surrounds the Childwall site so nothing of the set can really be seen. *Brookside* fans can see a slice of the close at a Liverpool Life exhibition at the city's Maritime Museum, where the inside of Ron Dixon's house has been recreated.

PRIDE AND PREJUDICE

Lyme Park, Cheshire

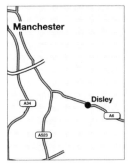

Jane Austen's comedy of manners *Pride and Prejudice* caused a sensation when it was screened on BBC1 in September and October 1995, and turned its two lead actors Colin Firth, who played Mr Darcy, and Jennifer Ehle, who played Elizabeth Bennet, into stars.

The story centres on Mrs Bennet, played by Alison Steadman, and her five daughters' pursuit of eligibly rich young men who come into their social world in 19th century Hertfordshire. The BBC's last version, adapted by Fay Weldon and screened in 1980, had been studio based, but the six-part 1995 version, adapted by award-winning screenwriter Andrew Davies, featured some of Britain's most stunning houses and countryside.

For the purposes of filming, Mr Darcy's stunning home Pemberley is quite a distance from Derbyshire, where it is supposed to be, and the exterior shots were actually filmed at beautiful Lyme Park in Cheshire. Lyme Park, one of the largest houses in the county, is owned by The National Trust and was the home of the Legh family for 600 years. It is open to the public most of the year. Telephone (01663) 762023 for more details.

Interior shots for Pemberley were actually closer to where they should have been, and they were filmed at late

17th century Sudbury Hall in Derbyshire, which is again owned by The National Trust. For more details telephone: (01283) 585305.

The Bennet family home, Longbourn was actually Luckington Court near Chipping Sodbury in Wiltshire. The house is privately owned and not open to the public, however the gardens are open on Wednesdays from 2-5pm. For further details telephone: (01666) 840205.

Just fifteen miles away is the beautiful village of Lacock, which is owned by The National Trust, and played Meryton on screen. The village dates back to the 13th century, and its limewashed half-timbered and stone houses also featured in ITV dramatisations of *Moll Flanders* and *Emma*. The production team filming *Moll Flanders* managed to upset the locals by using tonnes of soil to cover up the modern tarmac. Torrential rain later the same day then washed several inches of mud all down the main street!

There is also a 13th century abbey and museum to William Fox Talbot, inventor of the modern photographic negative at Lacock. For further details about the Abbey telephone: (01249) 730227 and the museum (01249) 730459.

'Even though it's a very pretty place, there were still scores of things we had to do to dress it properly,' says Gerry Scott, Production Designer on *Pride and Prejudice*. 'Contemporary shop fronts had to be covered or altered, many of the doors were covered with modern-day gloss paint, and others had the wrong type of knocker or bell-push.

'We had to go to the people who live there and say,

"Look, do you mind if…?" and without exception everyone was very kind and allowed us to tinker with their property.'

The ballroom at Brocket Hall, Welwyn, Hertfordshire, was used for the main ball held at Netherfield. The ballroom, which is now an upmarket conference venue, is 60 feet long and cost £1,500 when it was furnished in 1760. The mirrors are by Chippendale and the ceilings were painted by Sir Francis Wheatley, and it can be hired for private parties. It was in the ballroom at the dinner table that Lady Caroline Lamb famously arranged for herself to be served as a surprise dish at Lord Melbourne's birthday dinner, emerging naked from a large tureen. For details see the Brocket Hall website at http://www.brocket-hall.co.uk/

The other scenes at Netherfield were filmed at Edgecote Hall near Banbury in Oxfordshire, but it is privately owned and not open to the public. Rosings, home of Lady Catherine, was played by Belton House at Grantham, Lincolnshire. Belton, which was built in the late 17th century, is also now owned by The National Trust and is open for much of the year. For further details telephone: (01476) 566116. Details of all National Trust properties can be found on the internet at http://www.nationaltrust.org.uk/

Other scenes were filmed outside the Lord Leycester Hospital in Warwick, and the Lambton Inn was in Chapel Street, Longnor, Staffordshire. Jane Austen's real house is now a museum and is located in the village of Chawton near Alton in Hampshire. For details telephone: (01420) 83262. The writer's grave can be found in Winchester Cathedral.

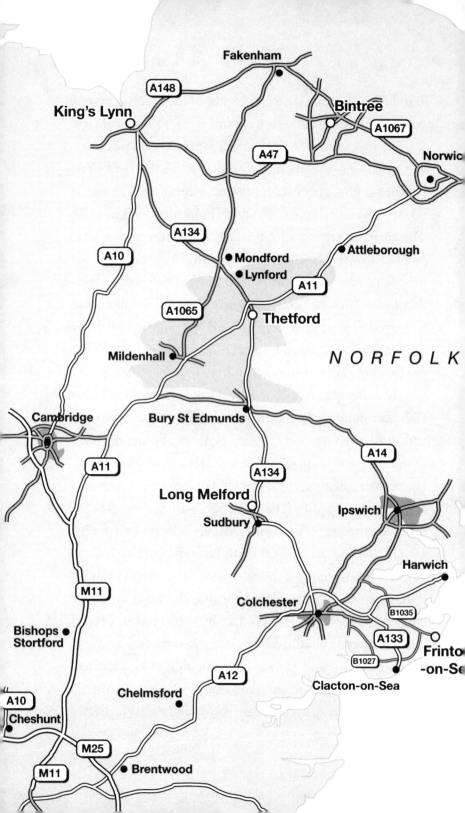

EAST ANGLIA

'ALLO, 'ALLO

Lynford Hall, Lynford, Norfolk

The BBC found the ideal location to play wartime France in 'Allo, 'Allo, the popular comedy about French resistance fighters. For Lynford Hall, at Lynford in Norfolk, was designed in the neo-Gothic style along the lines of a French château. The fact that Lynford Hall – built between 1857 and 1862 to replace the former Hall which stood around 300 yards away from the present site – wasn't too far from London made it the perfect double for France – and saved the BBC having to use a real French location.

Above: Filming at Lynford Hall, the location for *'Allo, 'Allo.*

Designed by William Burn, the Hall was built by Stephen Lyne-Stephen for his wife Pauline Duverney, a celebrated French ballerina, and the aim of the French-style design of the building was to make her feel less homesick. It worked to a degree, although she still spent much of her time in Paris and at her other home, Grove House at Roehampton.

The sight of uniforms was nothing new to the Hall,

as it had been used during both World Wars as a convalescent hospital for wounded officers. It was bought by Gerald Rand, a retired civil engineer and master builder, and in 1970 he embarked on a major restoration programme which took twenty years to restore the Hall to its former glory.

Lynford Hall was perfect for *'Allo, 'Allo* for two reasons. Firstly, the front of the main part of the building was ideal to play Gestapo officer Herr Flick's château headquarters, and secondly, the cobbled courtyard round the back was easily turned into the fictional town square of Novienne, including the focal point of the show, Café René. The BBC production team built the front of the Café and other Novienne shops over the front of the archways, which at the time were being used as garages and motel rooms. And, as with so many exterior locations, we never saw past the doorway as the inside shots were filmed in a studio elsewhere.

In later episodes of the show a replica of the outside set was built at the BBC's Elstree Studios but it was Lynford Hall that gave *'Allo, 'Allo* its original French feel. In addition to *'Allo, 'Allo*, Lynford Hall has also been used for scenes in *Dad's Army* and *You Rang M'Lord?*

In 1997 the Hall was bought by businessmen Peter Scopes and Tad Zlotek who have spent £2 million refurbishing it and turning it into a prestigious hotel and conference centre. It also has a licence for civil marriages and specialises in organic food and drink. Further details on Lynford Hall are available by telephoning (01842) 878351.

DAD'S ARMY

Thetford, Norfolk

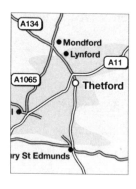

A German invasion force would have been completely foiled if it had tried to find Walmington-on-Sea, where Captain Mainwaring led his Home Guard Platoon in the BBC comedy *Dad's Army*. Although Walmington-on-Sea was supposed to be a small town on the coast in Sussex, the whole series was filmed in and around the Norfolk town of Thetford and its nearby environs.

Producers were lucky from the start because the Ministry of Defence agreed to allow them to use the Stanford Battle Area, a large training area requisitioned by the army during the war and still owned by the Ministry of Defence, a few miles from Thetford. 'We used to go there a lot because it was quiet and peaceful for filming – they had roads and everything, and we didn't get bothered by the public,' explains *Dad's Army* co-creator Jimmy Perry OBE. Bill Pertwee, who played Air Raid Warden Hodges in the series and has written a highly successful book about the show called *Dad's Army: The Making Of A Television Legend*, adds: 'We used it for a tremendous amount of locations, basically anything that involved chasing across fields, like the episode with the barrage balloon, "The Day The Balloon Went Up"'.

The cast and crew used to stay at the Bell Hotel and at the Anchor Hotel in Thetford. The streets of the town were used for filming and The Guildhall doubled as Walmington Town Hall in the episode 'The Captain's Car'. Residents were often asked to put masking tape across their windows, as they did during the war to stop flying glass, and happily got involved.

During filming of the series' eighty episodes between 1968 and 1977, dozens of locations all over Norfolk were used. 'We went all over the place,' says Jimmy Perry, 'and used to cover the whole of Norfolk.'

The pier at Great Yarmouth was used for the episode 'Menace From The Deep', and a disused airfield near Diss was also utilised. Sherringham railway station, which is now a preserved line and part of North Norfolk Railway Company, was used for an episode called 'The Royal Train'. The Norfolk Broads were used for an episode called 'Sons of the Sea'. Another memorable episode, 'The Two And A Half Feathers', which saw the whole cast playing out a long desert scene, was filmed at large sandpits at King's Lynn.

Drinkstone Mill at Drinkstone, Suffolk was used for the episode 'Don't Forget the Diver'. Just over the county boundary into Norfolk is Wacton, setting for the episode 'Round and Round Went The Big Wheel'. Santon Downham was the site of the bridge used in 'Brain Versus Brawn', and the next stop, Brandon Station is the railway station used in 'The Big Parade'. A National Trust castle, Oxburgh Hall, was used as Peabody Museum in 'Museum Piece'.

Lynford Hall was used as the backdrop to the shooting

range in 'Wake Up Walmington', an episode which also featured the Six Bells, a pub in Bardwell, which reappeared in the episode 'Ring Dem Bells'.

Not strictly a television location, but one of interest to fans of *Dad's Army*, is the pretty village of Chalfont St Giles in Buckinghamshire, which was used as the setting for the excellent 1971 *Dad's Army* feature film.

Members of The *Dad's Army* Appreciation Society have staged tours of all these locations and more. It costs £6 a year to join and details can be obtained by writing to Jack Wheeler, 8 Sinodun Road, Wallingford, Oxfordshire OX10 8AA.

LOVEJOY

Long Melford, Suffolk

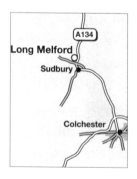

You might not bump into that lovable rogue Lovejoy if you head to Long Melford in Suffolk, but you will find scores of genuine antique shops full of the sort of stuff Lovejoy would love to get his hands on. Long Melford, so named because of its particularly long high street, which is three miles long, was one of around a dozen locations in Suffolk regularly used for filming *Lovejoy*, the highly successful BBC series which starred Ian McShane as the eponymous antique dealer. The

Above: Lady Jane's 'home' – actually Belchamp Hall, at Belchamp Walter.

attractive 16th century Bull Hotel was regularly featured in the series along with many of the village's antique shops, including Neptune Antiques and Ringer's Yard.

Over at Belchamp Walter, opposite the beautiful 15th century village church with mediaeval wall paintings, is Belchamp Hall, an elegant Queen Anne redbrick house, which was used as Lady Jane's home, Felsham Hall, in the series. The Hall is also available for hire for conferences, weddings and parties, and is open for tours on Tuesdays and Thursdays from May to September by appointment. For details telephone: 01787 881961 or see its website at http://www.belchamphall.com

The attractive 300-year-old thatched Half Moon pub at nearby Belchamp St Paul was a familiar sight in the autumn 1993 series of *Lovejoy* when it became one of his locals. Elsewhere, many other towns and villages in the area were regularly used in the series including Braintree, Hadleigh, Kersey, Lavenham, Felsham, Sudbury, Halstead, Bildeston and Bury St Edmunds, and all are interesting places to visit in addition to their *Lovejoy* locations. For example, Lavenham has a historic Guildhall and a market place which was used for filming.

THE MILL ON THE FLOSS

Bintree, Norfolk

The BBC's 1997 adaptation of George Eliot's classic tale of unrequited love which starred Emily Watson, James Frain and Bernard Hill, who went on to play Captain Smith in the blockbuster film *Titanic*, featured a number of stunning locations.

To find the principal location, that of the Dorlcote Mill, Location Manager Jeremy Johns visited 50 water-mills all over the country from Devon to the Lake District and from Wales to East Anglia. 'The main criterion was that it had to be picturesque with as few modern additions as possible. From a short-list of three mills in Norfolk, Warwickshire and Dorset, we finally decided upon Bintree Mill in Norfolk which was a real find.' It was ideal because it is set in a green belt valley with very few telephone and electricity cables, not in the middle of a village. 'When we found most of the film's other settings and locations in the vicinity, Bintree was a winner,' adds Jeremy. The interiors of Dorlcote the corn-loft, milling-floor and sack chute were found in another mill 16 miles away in Burgh-next-Aylsham, and the kitchen and parlour interiors were filmed in an old farmhouse in Salle.

Nearby were the locations for Lawyer Wakem's house and Lucy Deane's house, whilst the flood and rowing scenes were shot on a lake near Bintree.

MARTIN CHUZZLEWIT

King's Lynn, Norfolk

Written in 1843, Charles Dickens' sixth novel called for a labyrinth of tiny streets, supposedly in early 19th century London, and the BBC found the perfect location in the Norfolk town of King's Lynn. The story centres on an inheritance and the contrasting destinies of the wealthy brothers Chuzzlewit, and featured an all-star cast including Sir John Mills, Paul Schofield, Keith Allen, Tom Wilkinson and Julia Sawalha.

King's Lynn was one of England's foremost ports as

early as the 12th century, and even today late mediaeval merchants houses stretch back to the river between cobbled lanes and the famous Custom House. Those tiny streets proved to be perfect for the production team, and where there were modern road markings mud was used to cover them up. King's Lynn Council's offices doubled as Mrs Todgers' boarding houses, and the frontages of cottages at King's Straithe, which also played early New York in the film *Revolution*, were used extensively.

Elsewhere, St Margaret's House and the lane next door appeared, as did the back of King's Street. 'King's Lynn offered us the labyrinth of tiny streets that Dickens mentions in the novel,' says Production Designer Gavin Davies. 'I could get seven important locations within ten minutes of one another. Doing it in London would have been difficult if not downright impossible because of noise and traffic. We were able to close roads in King's Lynn without disrupting the whole town.'

The Fleece Inn, a 14th century pub in the Worcestershire village of Bretforton, appeared as The Blue Dragon, and a National Trust property Peckover House in Cambridgeshire played Mortague Tigg's home. Honington Hall, a 17th century house at Shipston-on-Stour, Warwickshire, also appeared. The house, which has also featured in *Our Mutual Friend* and *Keeping Up Appearances*, is open to the public on Wednesdays only from June to August from 2.30 - 5pm and at other times by appointment. For further details telephone: (01608) 661434.

HI-DE-HI

Warner's Holiday Camp, Dovercourt, near Frinton-on-Sea, Essex

The BBC comedy *Hi-De-Hi*, set in a 1950s holiday camp, was another huge hit from the script-writing partnership of Jimmy Perry and David Croft. Jimmy Perry had first-hand experience of life in a holiday camp, having worked as a Butlin's Redcoat many years ago. And using his memories of events and characters, he and David were able to introduce a fine blend of likeable characters which made the show an instant hit when it began in 1981, and it ran for eight years.

It was popular with the public, but holiday giants Butlins were less than impressed and refused to let the BBC use one of their holiday camps for filming. They had spent years, not to mention thousands of pounds in advertising, trying to shake off the old-fashioned holiday camp image which *Hi-De-Hi* re-created. 'Butlins didn't want to have anything to do with it,' says Jimmy Perry. 'They said: "We're spending half a million pounds on getting rid of the holiday camp image and you're bringing it back," so they weren't too interested!'

Fortunately another company, Warners, had no such objections to the show and allowed the BBC to film at their holiday camp at Dovercourt, near Frinton-on-Sea.

'It was a bit old-fashioned, which was great because we wanted somewhere that was a bit old,' says Jimmy. 'But it was very popular and was flourishing at the time we were there, and people loved to go there.'

Filming began at the camp a week after the last campers left, either the last week in September or the first week of October. By that time the weather had usually begun to get chilly and the cast would frequently complain about the cold. And with some justification, as they were often sporting just shorts and T-shirts for scenes that were supposed to be set at the height of summer but were actually being filmed in the middle of winter.

Actor Jeffery Holland – who starred in the series alongside Paul Shane, Ruth Madoc, Su Pollard and, for several early series, Simon Cadell – was one of those to come off worse. As camp funnyman Spike Dixon, he regularly had to be thrown into the infamous 'Olympic-size' swimming pool.

So many of Jeffery's memories of *Hi-De-Hi* involve being very cold and wet. 'I remember a very unpleasant day where I had to end up in the pool,' he recalls. 'I was dressed in a bathing suit with balloons and a blonde wig. Normally I used to wear a wetsuit under whatever costume I had on, but on this occasion there was nowhere to hide the wetsuit.

'So I got thrown in the water and it was the middle of October and it was so cold that my legs started to go numb and I had to get out. I knew if I didn't get out they'd have had to pull me out and I might not have finished the series!'

Ruth Madoc, who played Chief Yellowcoat, Gladys Pugh, also recalls: 'It was always very chilly, I can't remember it ever being boiling hot. We used to have to wear thermal underwear!' Sadly we'll never hear Ruth Madoc's voice over the Maplin's tannoy again, as the holiday camp is no more. It was bulldozed several years ago.

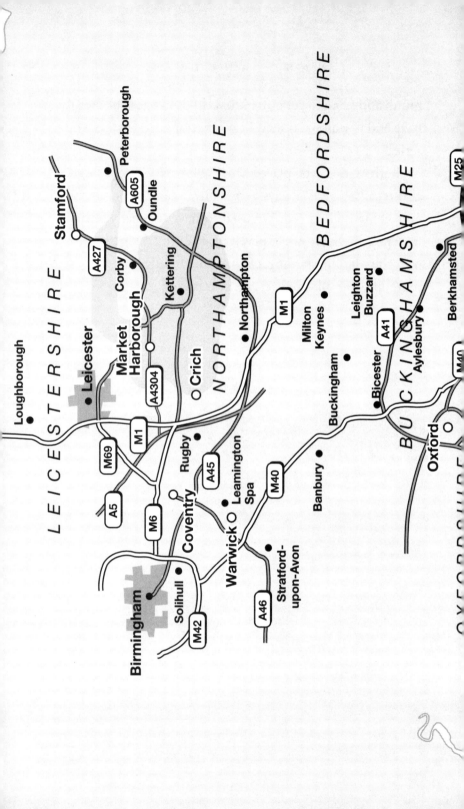

THE MIDLANDS

PEAK PRACTICE

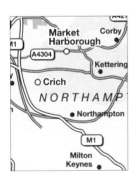

Peak Practice has become one of ITV's most successful drama series of the past decade. It began in 1993 when it starred Kevin Whately as Dr Jack Kerruish, Amanda Burton as Dr Beth Glover and Simon Shepherd as Dr Will Preston. Over the years the faces at The Beeches surgery in the fictional village of Cardale have changed, but the story goes on and the 1999 line-up features Gary Mavers as Dr Andrew Attwood and Haydn Gwynne as Dr Joanna Graham.

The pretty Derbyshire village of Crich plays Cardale, and before you even reach Crich marketplace you'll spot on your left, down the hill next to the Black Swan pub, Archway House which played Dr Beth Glover's home.

Next you'll see Crich Foodmarket, which doubles as the bank in the series, and a few doors along from that is the local fish and chip shop run by John and Phyl Cousins, which is now called The Cardale Fish and Chip Shop. The series' cast and crew often visit the shop while filming, and Kevin Whately, who used to play Dr Jack Kerruish, used to be a regular.

To find the house that played Dr Kerruish's home, take a left turn down Dimple Lane, go down for about a quarter of a mile until you see fields on your left, carry on further and you'll find Melkridge House. The cottage is actually available to rent as a holiday home through English Country Cottages. For further details telephone: (0870) 8581111.

Returning to the main road, turn left at the top of Dimple Lane and follow the road for about a mile until you see a sign marked Fritchley ¼ of a mile. Follow the sign and go down the hill until you find Bobbin Mill Hill. Go down Bobbin Mill Hill and up on a sharp right hand bend is Chesnut Bank, the large house which plays The Beeches surgery in the series.

The pub where Jack Kerruish got involved in a fight in an early episode of *Peak Practice* is actually The Manor Hotel, in nearby South Wingfield. Close by is Wingfield Manor, a ruined mansion now owned by English Heritage, was used for Cardale's mediaeval pageant. For details about the manor, which was also used for Franco Zeffirelli's 1996 film *Jane Eyre*, telephone: (01773) 833287.

The church where Dr Erica Matthews jilted Dr Andrew Attwood during the 1998 series was St Peter's Church at Edensor inside Chatsworth Park. Dr David Shearer was hit and killed by a motorcycle at Elton and the funeral was filmed at St Giles Church at Hartington. Outside Crich, locations all round the beautiful Peak District and in the magnificent Peak District National Park are regularly used.

Below: The Beeches Surgery from *Peak Practice*.

VANITY FAIR

Set during the Napoleonic Wars, William Makepeace Thackeray's classic novel *Vanity Fair* follows the life of Becky Sharp, the penniless, orphaned daughter of an artist and a French opera dancer, and Amelia Sedley, the sheltered child of a rich city merchant. The pair are unlikely but firm friends, but very different in character. Becky is an irresistible schemer and will stop at nothing to get what she wants, whereas Amelia is meek and mild and pursues the opposite course.

The lavish 1998 BBC adaptation of *Vanity Fair* starred Natasha Little as Becky, Frances Grey as Amelia, Nathaniel Parker as red-blooded Rawdon Crawley and Tom Ward as dashing officer George Osborne. The series took 21 weeks to film and was shot in locations as diverse as London, Paris, the Rhine Valley and the west coast of Wales.

The ballroom scene was filmed at Cheltenham Town Hall, and the town's Pittville Pump Room was used as a foreign restaurant for another scene. Both are open to the public and part of the Pump Room is now a museum.

The beach and several rows of houses in Tenby, Wales doubled as Brighton, and Ragley Hall, Warwickshire, played the home of Lord Steyne.

Claydon House at Middle Claydon, Buckinghamshire also featured, playing the interior of a hotel in Germany. It is owned by the National Trust and is open to the public. For details telephone: (01296) 730349.

Stowe Landscape Gardens at Buckingham, Buckinghamshire, a stunning survivor of Georgian times, doubled as Hyde Park. For more details telephone: (01280) 822850. The nearby house is now a school, but some rooms can be visited.

KEEPING UP APPEARANCES

Coventry

Driving instructor Tony Healey has become quite used to being called Mr Bucket by schoolchildren as they walk past his house in the Coventry suburb of Binley Wood.

For Tony and his wife Rosemary live on Heather Road, which plays the home of social climber Hyacinth Bucket (or Bouquet as she pronounces it) and her put-upon husband Richard, in the hit BBC comedy series *Keeping Up Appearances*.

'The schoolchildren give me some lip,' Tony reveals. 'Quite often when they come past I'm cleaning the windows of my car and I've got a bucket in my hand and they say: "It's Mr Bucket!" And some of the neighbours we're really friendly with will make one or two comments, but it's all in fun. I've been called Mr Bucket on quite a number of occasions, and sometimes friends will phone me up and say: "Is that the Bouquet residence?"'

When the *Keeping Up Appearances* location manager turned up on Tony's doorstep and asked if they could use the outside of the house for filming, Tony thought it was a joke. Their neighbours had already agreed to let the BBC use their home as the Buckets' neighbours Elizabeth and Emmet's house. 'The location manager said they'd been searching for a long while to find the right houses, and so we agreed to let them use ours.'

But after filming had begun, Tony wasn't sure he'd made the right decision. "After they first came I regretted it for a while because they brought such a lot of people – there were 40, 50, sometimes 60 crew and they blocked the road. They brought electrical equipment and generator vans and I felt a bit conscious about the neighbours, but they gradually got it better and now they disperse the vehicles and don't bring so many crew with them.'

Before the BBC start filming, they cover the window of Tony's garage with polystyrene shutters and put down a plastic sheet with real plants as a fake garden by the side of the garage. More plants are added to the existing border by the fence. 'They fill the border flowers and other stuff in pots which are hidden,' says Tony. 'And last time they were here they left us three hanging baskets.'

The BBC also put polystyrene shutters by the other windows and put up net curtains so Tony and Rosemary can't be seen while they are filming, which can start as early as 7am and not end until 6pm. Tony and Rosemary even let Patricia Routledge, who plays Hyacinth, use their dining room as her make-up room. Says Tony: 'She's a nice woman and keeps herself to herself to a certain degree; they all do.'

Tony and Rosemary, who have lived in Heather Road for 14 years, have spent the money the BBC has paid them on the house. 'We had a new garden wall put up because it was in a bit of a state,' says Tony.

Below: The Bucket residence from *Keeping Up Appearances.*

Despite his home having a starring role in the series in all the exterior scenes and shots filmed from the hallway, Tony admits he isn't a fan. 'I don't normally watch it,' he says. 'It doesn't interest me. I occasionally see it just to see what the front of the house looks like at certain times of the year, but I'm not a fan. It's not my sort of programme.'

Tony prefers another series by *Keeping Up Appearances* writer Roy Clarke, *Last Of The Summer Wine*. 'I find that more funny than this,' says Tony who prefers instead to continue with his hobby of restoring vintage motorcycles. Rosemary does enjoy the show, although, as she says: 'I prefer the other family, I find them amusing. Hyacinth is too over the top for me.'

People often recognise the house from the television but few knock on the door. Says Tony: 'We quite often see a car come past. The people stop, have a look, smile and then drive off again. We've only had two or three people come to the door and ask me if this is the house on the television.'

A few miles away, on a council estate in Coventry, is Michell Close where number three plays the home of Hyacinth's sister Daisy and her husband Onslow. The house was chosen because there is a scrapyard at the end of the road which is used as Onslow's Yard.

DANGERFIELD

Warwick, Warwickshire

The BBC drama which stars Nigel Havers as police surgeon Dr Jonathan Paige and Jane Gurnett as Detective Inspector Gillian Cramer is filmed in and around the beautiful town of Warwick, which is dominated by magnificent Warwick Castle.

The key location for the show is Dr Paige's surgery, and if it looks authentic that's because it is, as the exterior scenes are filmed at the real-life surgery, The Old Dispensary in Castle Street, Warwick.

The first four series of the show starred Nigel Le Vaillant as Dr Paul Dangerfield, and his home for the first three series was played by a house on Shipston Road near Stratford-upon-Avon. For series four he moved to another house, played by The Malt House in Mill Street, Warwick.

The house that now plays Dr Paige's home is in Castle Street. For the first four series the real-life police stations at Leamington Spa and Warwick doubled as the police station, but regular noise interruptions to filming meant a new location, so the front of the Heart of England Building Society, Castle Lane, was used for the fifth series. St Mary's Church in the centre of Warwick was used for the wedding of Dr Dangerfield's daughter Alison.

All the interior shots for the police station, the surgery, Dr Paige's home and the mortuary are filmed on specially built sets in an industrial unit at Redditch. The production team used to use the real-life mortuary at Warwick Hospital but they could only film there after 4.30 on a Friday, which was inconvenient, and the film crew apparently couldn't stand the smell!

INSPECTOR MORSE

Oxford, Oxfordshire

There is very little of central Oxford that hasn't, at some time, appeared in *Inspector Morse*, the award-winning detective series which stars John Thaw as the thoughtful Oxford sleuth. Some landmarks are easily recognisable from the television, but others, notably the colleges, are more difficult because several different real locations were often used to make one fictional place.

The King's Arms, on the corner of Hollywell Street and Parks Road, is one of the easily identifiable places – and was used by Morse to down a few pints of his favourite Samuel Smith's best bitter in several episodes.

Just along in Hollywell Street is the Music Room, owned by Wadham College, which was used in the final episode of *Inspector Morse* where opera singer Gladys Probert, played by Sheila Gish, gave a masterclass.

Back in Broad Street is the bookshop, Blackwells,

where Morse was seen in several episodes buying books, and next door is the White Horse pub, another of Morse's favourite haunts.

On the other side of Broad Street is the impressive Sheldonian Theatre, where Oxford University confers its degrees. In *Morse* it was used in the episode 'Dead on Time' when Morse took his ex-fiancée Susan Fallon to a concert there. To the side of the Sheldonian Theatre, next door to the Bodleian Library lies the square used in 'Twilight of the Gods' where a shooting took place.

In Radcliffe Square, not far from Broad Street, is the unusually shaped Radcliffe Camera and next door to it is Brasenose College which appeared as two fictional colleges, Beaufort and Beaumont, in various episodes.

Seen from the beautiful Christchurch meadow is Merton College which appeared in the episode 'The Infernal Serpent'. Christchurch itself was used as the backdrop to several episodes, and is very noticeable because of its distinctive Tom Tower.

The porter's lodge at Pembroke College was used for the episode 'Deceived By Flight' when Sergeant Lewis (Kevin Whately) posed as a porter to catch a murderer and a smuggler. 'I think we've filmed at every college in Oxford that would have us,' says Location Manager Russell Lodge. 'And that's 90 per cent of them.'

Out of the city, at Wolvercote, is the delightful Trout pub which is on the bank of the River Isis. It was from the bridge next to the pub that Morse and Lewis watched a frogman recover the Anglo-Saxon belt buckle, the

Wolvercote Tongue, in the episode of the same name. The Randolph Hotel (telephone 01865 247481) in Beaumont Street also featured heavily in this episode and also appears in other stories. It's also regularly used by John Thaw when he stays in Oxford for filming, and when he appeared in the marvellous film *Shadowlands*.

Oxford isn't the only place used to film *Morse* – and in the episode 'Masonic Mysteries' none of the city was used. Although on-screen it looks as if Morse rarely leaves the city, usually only five days of filming out of twenty-five are done in the city, with the rest shot in other locations

doubling as Oxford. A territorial army centre in Southall, London, was used as the police station for the first two series, although for those series the front we saw on-screen was the front of the real Oxford police station.

For the third, fourth and fifth series a TA centre in Harrow played the police station and a Ministry Of Defence laboratory in Harefield in Hertfordshire did the same job in the sixth and seventh series, but was demolished in the spring of 1993.

The front of the police station was not shown that

Below: John Thaw signs autographs for fans.

much on-screen as Morse and Lewis mainly used the back entrance. Morse's home is actually miles from Oxford. It is a ground floor flat in a Victorian block in Castlebar Road, Ealing. When Morse's home caught fire in one episode, a set of the flat was built in a studio and burned, although fake smoke came through a broken window at the real flat. It was filmed there because it was cheaper not to travel to Oxford, and it doesn't involve an expensive overnight stay for the actors and crew. In fact, many of the streets in Ealing look very similar to houses on the Woodstock or Banbury roads out of Oxford.

Another of Morse's favourite pubs, which was supposed to be near Oxford, was actually filmed at The Crown at Bray in Berkshire. 'We used the inside a lot,' says Russell Lodge. 'We slightly decorated the inside by changing the pictures, and they are still up now.' The pub was picked because the *Morse* production team were filming at nearby Bray film studios.

Scenes for the recent story 'The Wench Is Dead', which saw actor Matthew Finney joining Morse as his new sidekick Adrian Kershaw instead of Lewis, was filmed at The Black Country Museum at Dudley, and on canals in Northamptonshire and Wiltshire.

The graveyard scenes – supposedly in Ireland – were filmed at Abersoch in Wales and a few extra fibreglass gravestones were added to real ones there. Morse spent most of the episode in Radcliffe Infirmary in Oxford and the scenes of him leaving were actually filmed there.

BY THE SWORD DIVIDED

Rockingham Castle, Market Harborough, Leicestershire

Location managers could hardly have found a better location than Rockingham Castle for the BBC's 1983 series *By The Sword Divided*. Set in 1640 during the English Civil War, the series followed the lives of the Royalist Lacey family and documented their involvement in the conflict. It starred Julian Glover as Sir Martin Lacey, Gold Blend ad girl Sharon Maughan as his daughter Anne Lacey, and Timothy Bentinck – famous on radio as David Archer in *The Archers* – as his son Tom Lacey, and ran for two ten-part series.

Rockingham was perfect as Arnescote because it had real-life experiences of the Civil War when it was badly damaged, having had its Norman keep razed to the ground, its walls pocked by cannon and its pleasure gardens flattened. It has been in the Watson family since 1530. The first Lord Rockingham, Sir Lewis Watson, was a Royalist, but his wife Eleanor was a Parliamentarian. However, they agreed on one subject – that their home, with its keep and fortress wall which commanded views over four counties, was bound to be occupied by soldiers.

They expected Royalists to occupy Rockingham and Parliamentary forces to take nearby Belvoir Castle. Based

Right: The stunning Rockingham Castle, where *By The Sword Divided* was filmed.

on this theory they sent their gold and silver to Belvoir for safe-keeping. But Belvoir fell to the Royalists and Rockingham to the Parliamentarians. So the Watsons lost their property and valuables to both factions and Sir Lewis was first imprisoned by the Royalists for disloyalty, then fined £5,000 by the Commonwealth.

Charles Dickens was a frequent visitor during the 19th century, and he wrote a large portion of his novel *Bleak House* during his stays at the castle. He's also reputed to have seen Lady Dedlock's ghost behind the 400-year-old yew hedge.

More than three centuries after the Civil War, Rockingham, which is still owned by the Watson family, saw Cavalier and Roundhead battles once more when the BBC arrived. The film team added mock stone turrets, disguised post-Commonwealth features and covered modern roads with mushroom compost, but other than these superficial changes, Arnescote is Rockingham and what we saw on television more than a decade ago can be seen now.

Rockingham is open to the public from Easter Sunday until the third week in October on Sundays and Thursdays, Bank Holiday Mondays and the Tuesdays following, and also on Tuesdays during August from 1-5pm. In addition, visitors can see the castle at other times during the year by appointment. Further details: (01536) 770240.

MIDDLEMARCH

Stamford, Lincolnshire

Producers of the 1994 BBC serial *Middlemarch*, which starred Rufus Sewell as Will Ladislaw, Douglas Hodge as Tertius Lydgate and Juliet Aubrey as Dorothea Brooke, expected to film in many different towns in order to re-create Victorian England authentically.

Explains Producer Louis Marks: 'We presumed we'd have to film all over the country – a street here, a square there, a house somewhere else.

'But then our researchers came back and told us they'd found this marvellous town that had everything. So I went up to Lincolnshire, took one look and I knew they were right. Stamford is beautiful.'

The town needed some ageing, and period-style doors were placed over new ones and 'Georgian' windows were hung over the top of modern ones. Locations used in the town include unspoiled St George's Square, Browne's Hospital and the area Barn Hill – which includes number 3 All Saints Place, which played Doctor Lydgate's home.

Rambling Mill Lane and Stamford Arts Centre, which doubled as the White Hart Hotel, also appear. In fact, the Arts Centre, which also contains Stamford Tourist Information Centre, looked so much like a hotel after the

BBC film team decorated it that several visitors to the town during filming tried to book rooms!

Outside the town centre, Grimsthorpe Castle doubled as Qualingham. The castle, which was also used for scenes in *Moll Flanders* and *The Buccaneers*, is open from March 29th until September 27th on Sundays, Thursdays and Bank Holidays, and Sunday to Thursday from August 3rd to 31st. The Park and Gardens are open from 11am to 6pm, and the Castle is open from 2pm to 5pm. For more details telephone: (01778) 591205.

The carriage scenes in the opening episode were filmed at Burghley Park which is open to the public daily between Easter and early October from 8.30am to 8.30pm. For further details telephone: (01780) 752451 or look at the website: http://www.stamford.co.uk/burghley/

For further details about Stamford contact Stamford Tourist Information Office on: (01780) 755611 or look at the website http://www.stamford.co.uk

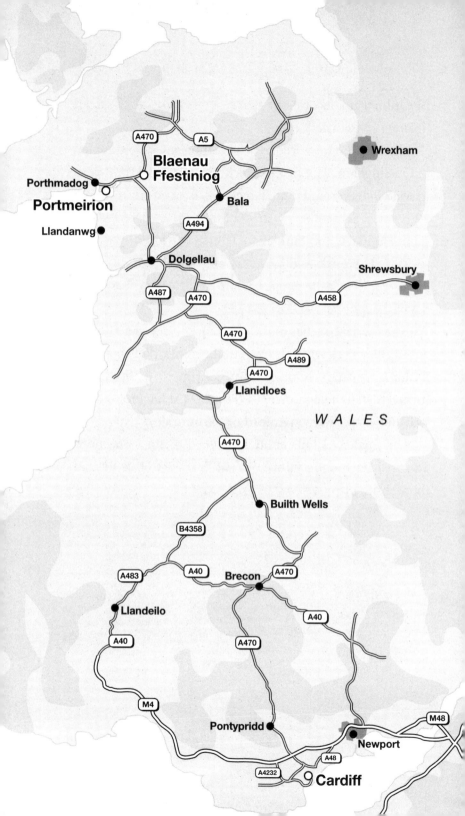

WALES

THE PRISONER

Portmeirion, Gwynedd

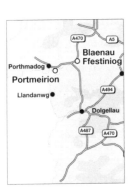

The cult 1960s series *The Prisoner* was filmed at the privately-owned Mediterranean-style village of Portmeirion in North Wales. The village is situated on top of a wooded clifftop, on its own private peninsula overlooking the Traeth Bach Estuary and Cardigan Bay. It is surrounded by sub-tropical woodlands known as Y Gwyllt, where rare and exotic species flourish in the frost-free climate. Miles of woodland paths meander among lakes and valleys to the beaches of White Sands Bay at the end of the peninsula.

The village was the inspiration of architect Sir Clough

Williams-Ellis who fell in love with the Italian fishing village of Portofino as a young man and resolved one day to create something as charming in Britain. During the early 1920s he began searching for a site for his dream but was beginning to give up hope after looking at two dozen islands around Britain. Then, in 1925, he was asked by an uncle if he could find a buyer for a small craggy, wooded peninsula, then called Aber Ia, situated between Harlech and Porthmadog. The site was terribly overgrown but once he saw it, Williams-Ellis realised his search was over.

Writing in his book, *Portmeirion*, which was first published in 1930, Williams-Ellis, who died in 1978, recalled his impression of the place: 'It has all and more – much more – than I had ever dreamed of as a desirable for my perfect site – beetling cliffs and craggy pinnacles, level plateaux and little valleys, a tumbling cascade, splendid old trees and exotic flowering shrubs; a coastline of rocky headlands, caves and sandy bays, and on top of it all, a sheltered harbour for my boat at the nearest possible point of the sea.'

Over the next few years Williams-Ellis converted the early Victorian house on the site into a luxury hotel and added cottages into his village as time and money allowed. He also travelled the country purchasing architecturally interesting but dilapidated buildings, set for demolition, which he brought to Portmeirion and rebuilt. Williams-Ellis himself called the place a 'home for fallen buildings'.

For example, the 17th century town hall, whose ceiling

Right: Portmeirion, the location for *The Prisoner*.

depicts the life and labours of Hercules, was rescued from demolition and taken to Portmeirion stone by stone and restored to its former glory. Williams-Ellis had spotted details of the building, Emral Hall at Worthenbury, in *Country Life* magazine and bought the ceilings for just £13. But he spent thousands bringing the whole building to Portmeirion.

The village, which became a popular place for visitors including Edward VIII, HG Wells, John Steinbeck and Nöel Coward, who wrote his play *Blithe Spirit* while staying at the hotel, was completed in 1973 and now comprises fifty buildings arranged around a central piazza.

Actor Patrick McGoohan discovered Portmeirion while filming an episode of his 60s spy series *Danger Man* in Wales. He realised it was the perfect location for a new series he'd been planning called *The Prisoner*, which showbiz mogul Lew Grade had agreed to finance with a then unheard-of budget of £75,000 an episode. The series followed the surreal adventures of an ex-spy with no name, just a number – Number Six – marooned in a strange village from which he would constantly try to escape. The 17-part series was a massive hit attracting around 12 million viewers each week. But the final episode upset the public – because it was inconclusive.

After it was shown, ITV switchboards were flooded by angry callers, McGoohan's London home was besieged, his children were hassled on their way home from school and McGoohan was, reportedly, physically attacked.

McGoohan recalls: 'We had to go and hide in Wales for a couple of weeks with no telephones.'

Today the series enjoys cult status and members of *The Prisoner* Appreciation Society, Six Of One, stage a yearly convention at Portmeirion where they re-enact episodes and play the famous Human Chess Game. McGoohan is delighted by the attention *The Prisoner* still enjoys. 'I think it's marvellous,' he says. 'If they understand it please pass on the understanding to me. I'd love to know what it's about!'

Portmeirion is open all year round and contains a number of shops including a Prisoner Six of One Information Centre. The hotel was gutted by fire in 1981, but has now been completely renovated and is a splendid place to stay. For further information telephone: (01766) 770228 or check out the Portmeirion website http://www.portmeirion.wales.com

OUR MUTUAL FRIEND

Cardiff

The Blitz and modern development caused a headache for the production team preparing to recreate 1860s London for the BBC's all-star 1998 version of the epic Charles Dickens novel *Our Mutual Friend*. The adaptation, a powerful portrait of London life which entwines two passionate love stories round an exploration of class tensions and new money, starred Paul McGann, Anna Friel, David Morrissey and Keeley Hawes.

They needed a sprawling warehouse on the riverfront overlooking the Thames at Southwark for filming, but there was no genuine site which adequately fitted the bill, so Location Manager Andy Jackson was forced to look elsewhere. Finally, after clocking up 8,000 miles on his car in a search for the right location to double as 1860s Southwark, and having rejected sites all over Britain, a colleague showed him some pictures of Cardiff Docks which, after building the warehouse set from scratch, would fit the bill.

Elsewhere, a disused stone quarry at Trifil, a few miles from Merthyr Tydfil, Wales was used and 17th century Honington Hall, Shipston-on-Stour, Warwickshire, played Mr and Mrs Boffin's home after they'd gained their wealth. It's open to the public on Wednesdays only from June to

August from 2.30-5pm and at other times by appointment. For further details telephone: (01608) 661434.

Scenes were filmed all over London including the English Speaking Union in Charles Street, which played the Veneerings' house and the Middle Temple, Lincoln's Inn Fields, Gun Street and Somerset House. The backstreet scenes behind the warehouses were filmed at Chatham Dockyard.

EDGE OF DARKNESS

Blaenau Ffestiniog

The award-winning BBC thriller *Edge of Darkness* saw Bob Peck playing Yorkshire detective Ronald Craven who was investigating the mysterious death of his daughter Emma. She'd been part of an ecology group and was killed after she discovered a secret nuclear plant, Northmoor, under the Welsh mountains.

In reality, Northmoor was a clever creation by BBC designers who built a whole complex underground at a disused slate mine at Manod, Blaenau Ffestiniog in North Wales. Offices were built, walkways constructed and miles of cable had to be run in for both working lights and lights for filming. And it was no easy task. To get to the entrance of the mine, which was dug into the side of a hill, meant driving cross-country for around two miles: it took the production team around six weeks to complete their set building work. It involved carrying the whole set miles underground as vehicles could only go into the mine for the first ½ mile.

'The passageways were very narrow and we had to light them all ourselves,' recalls Mike Bartley, Production Associate on the project. 'It was very tricky and quite a dangerous place and it went on for miles and miles.' Once inside, the mine opened out into a huge cave which had been used during the last war to store valuable paintings.

The entrance used by Ronald Craven and maverick CIA officer Darius Jedburgh to enter Northmoor was actually shot at a gold mine at Dolgellau, one of the last in Britain. On screen we saw Craven and Jedburgh enter the mine and dodge passing underground railway trucks and then the action cuts back to the Manod mine. The nearby Llechwedd slate mine at Blaenau Ffestiniog is open to the public. For details telephone: (01766) 830522.

Other than Wales, the headquarters of Yorkshire Police at Bradford was used as Craven's police station and his home was a house at Ilkley. The programme's conference sequence in the last episode was filmed at Gleneagles in Scotland and not far away was the lodge used for the final shoot-out scenes.

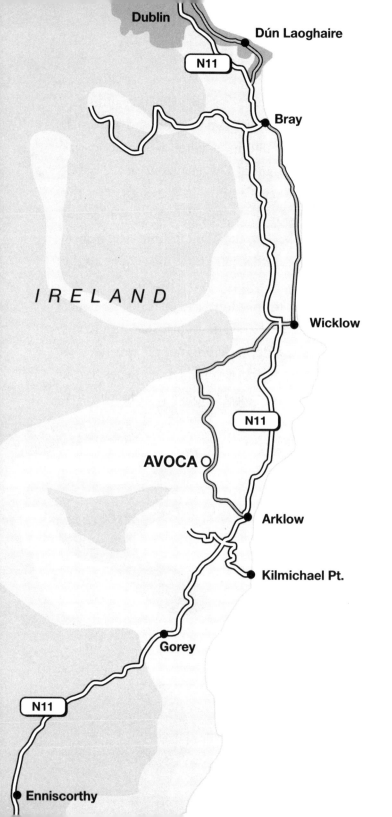

IRELAND

BALLYKISSANGEL

Avoca, County Wicklow

The town of Avoca, in County Wicklow, which doubles on screen as the sleepy village of Ballykissangel, is actually in the Republic of Ireland. It is included in this book simply because of the popularity of the BBC series and because it is within easy reach of the UK.

The series began in 1996, and saw rookie English priest Father Peter Clifford, played by Stephen Tompkinson, arrive to take on a new job as the local curate. He became friends with local bar owner Assumpta, played by Dervla Kirwan, and soon wised up to the ways of the locals. He faced ongoing battles with his immediate superior, wily old parish priest Father MacAnally, played by Niall Toibin, and local businessman Brian Quigley, played by Tony Doyle. After two series both Stephen and Dervla decided to quit the show and two new characters – Orla O'Connell, played by Victoria Smurfit and Sean Dillon, played by Lochan Cranitch – were introduced to fill the gap, and the series remains ever popular.

The real-life locals of Avoca have been delighted with the success of the show and the influx of visitors it has brought them. Bernie Ivers runs a local guesthouse which became home to a number of the cast during filming. 'Ballykissangel is very good,' he says. 'The filming is important to our local economy.' Local publican Peter Moore agrees. 'We are largely dependent on tourism,' he says. 'And this can only help.'

Stephen Tompkinson was surprised by the number of tourists the show attracted to Avoca. 'It was amazing,' he says. 'We had as many as 20 coachloads a day passing through when we were filming in the summer, plus all the people in cars, but they were all very good about letting us get on with it.'

Almost all the interior scenes for *Ballykissangel* – apart from Hendley's shop, which you can visit and where you can buy *Ballykissangel* souvenirs, and the church – are filmed in studios near Dublin, but there's still plenty to see in Avoca. First stop might be Fitzgerald's, formerly The Fountain Bar, which plays Fitzgerald's on-screen and where you're bound to get a warm welcome, and nearby is Fitzgerald's Craft which sells a range of Avoca and *Ballykissangel* souvenirs.

About 100 yards up the road is St Mary and St Patrick Church, which doubles as St Joseph's. Then there is the post office, which is a tea-room and is borrowed by the BBC for filming, as the real post office, across the river, isn't used.

The locations for Quigley's House and Father Mac's are actually in Enniskerry, about 30 miles away. For more details contact The Irish Tourist Board on (0171) 518 0800 or see the web pages: http://www.avoca.com http://www.wicklow.ie or http://www.ireland.travel.ie

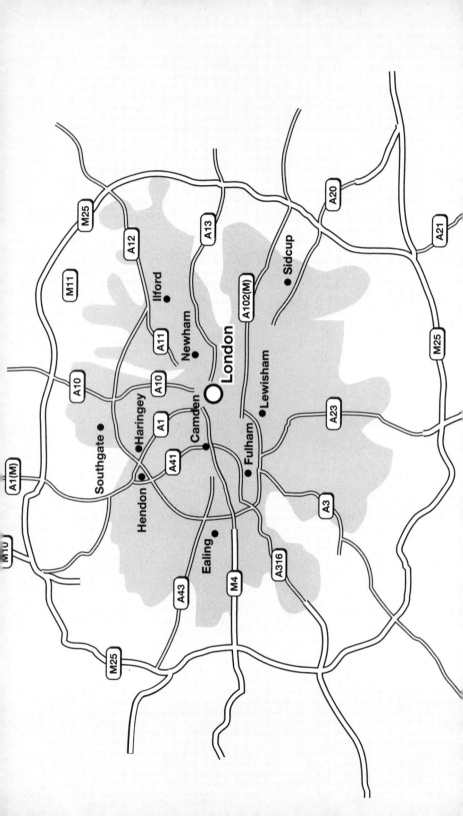

LONDON

LONDON'S BURNING

Dockhead Fire Station,
Wolseley Street

Real-life Dockhead Fire Station is used as the fictional Blackwall Station in *London's Burning* and plays home to Sicknote, George, Recall and the rest of the Blue Watch crew.

For the original 1986 90-minute *London's Burning* film, from which the highly successful series began, the whole of the Dockhead Fire Station was used for filming. London Weekend Television had full co-operation from the London Fire Brigade and the production team put porta-cabins in the station yard for the real fire-fighters for the six-week duration of the filming. The portacabins were used to replace the fire-fighter's relaxation area, canteen, mess and sleeping quarters while their real equivalents were being used for filming.

In exchange for allowing the production team to use their mess area, the fire-fighters were given free meals with the cast and crew in the catering bus. Fortunately for everyone involved things have become far simpler since those days. The production team has built a full-scale replica of the upper floor of Dockhead Fire Station, including the kitchen, mess, dormitories, rest room, shower room and offices, at Long Lane Studios in London.

And, of course, there is also the famous fire-fighters' pole, although the replica is just 7 foot long compared with the real pole at Dockhead which measures 18 foot. The set is on the ground floor, so although the pole room doors are there, the pole doesn't go anywhere.

The *London's Burning* team still film all their exterior shots at Dockhead using the yard at the front and the back and the appliance bay. Because Dockhead is a busy working fire station the first priority of the film team is making sure they are never in the way when the real fire-fighters head out on a 'shout'. 'We shoot it on the basis that it's a working station so as soon as the bells go down we get out of the way,' says *London's Burning* Location Manager Kevin Holden. 'And if, in fact, we need to put our own appliances in the appliance bays then the real fire appliances go into the courtyard in front so they are always

Right: Stars of *London's Burning* old and new.

on standby and the fire-fighters are always able to get in and drive them straight out.

'That's the prime concern – filming is one thing but we wouldn't want to be responsible for holding up a fire engine. That's the basis on which we do it and, of course, we've now been doing it for quite a long time so we're all used to it. We don't wait for the fire-fighters to come down the pole before we actually get out of the way.'

Dozens of locations all over London and the surrounding counties have been used for *London's Burning.* Quite often locations are used outside London although they are meant to be portraying the capital. For example, a multi-car pile-up on a major London road was filmed on an unopened stretch of the A3 at Liss in Hampshire. Other locations used include the Thames Barrier, the London Fire Brigade Museum at Southwark, and Surrey Docks in Southeast London, which was used in the episode where Vaseline drowned. Among the locations used for the 1993 series are two former military establishments, the former cruise missile base at Greenham Common in Berkshire and the Royal Marines Barracks at Eastney in Portsmouth.

Even Downing Street featured in one episode when campaigning fire-fighter Sicknote, played by Richard Walsh, handed a petition in to Prime Minister Margaret Thatcher at Number Ten. 'We shot the scene at the gates to Downing Street,' recalls Kevin. 'We weren't able to go into Downing Street. The only show, I believe, that has been able to film in Downing Street itself since they put the gates up was *Yes, Prime Minister* and that was because it was Margaret Thatcher's favourite programme, or so rumour has it!'

THE BILL

London

Television's best known police station Sun Hill has actually been at three locations in the capital. When *The Bill* began in 1984, the production base was at a single-storey office and warehouse complex in Artichoke Hill, Wapping in East London.

By 1986 the production had over-grown the Wapping site and plans to make the series twice weekly had necessitated a move to bigger premises. And the dispute between nearby News International and the print unions had become a problem as the police often blocked off roads in the area. And so a red-brick, former record company distribution warehouse in Barlby Road, North Kensington became Sun Hill number two. The Victorian building, with an arched doorway, was well suited to its role and became a popular home for the series with both the actors and the production team.

When Thames TV's lease on the building ran out in 1989, the owners announced that they were going to turn the site into a shopping precinct and members of *The Bill*'s production team had no other choice than to look for a new home for the show. Finding a new base for the set – and all the production suites – proved far from easy, but

Above: On location with *The Bill*.

eventually Thames decided upon a former wine warehouse in a suburb in Southwest London.

Producing two episodes of the series per week was never easy at the best of times, but trying to move a whole set and carry on filming at the same time was a mammoth logistical task. Extra episodes were stockpiled, which involved making three a week for a number of months. They helped to cover the period when no filming could take place while the new set was being completed.

And, of course, there was another consideration – how to 'move' Sun Hill on-screen without leaving viewers wondering why the now-familiar Sun Hill police station suddenly looked different. This was done by writing a modernisation of the fictional station into the storyline. This allowed for portacabins, scaffolding and junk to be strewn around the exterior of the station to cover the move. And the writers had another trick up their sleeves – they wrote an episode in which a huge car bomb blew up part of the station killing popular PC Ken Melvin (played by Mark Powley).

The new – and current – set was bigger than the two previous ones and extra sections were added to allow the filming of three episodes a week which began in the autumn of 1992. In addition, there are extensive areas for editing, casting, forward planning, costume, and a garage to store all the vehicles in. A courtroom and a hospital set for the fictional St Hugh's Casualty Unit were added to make filming easier and quicker than travelling to real locations, and the St Hugh's set was expanded in early 1999.

The Bill is unusual amongst television productions in that all the studios are real buildings. Most television sets are three-sided allowing room for a camera team. *The Bill*'s offices and cells are all real solid areas which look just like the real thing both on-and off-screen.

Sadly, *The Bill* is not able to welcome visitors for tours of the set due to the fact that there is always filming taking place somewhere in the building. And outside the studios there aren't really any regular locations used by the show, as filming is deliberately done all over South and West London.

The cast of *The Bill* enjoy a
Christmas knees-up.

YOU RANG M'LORD?

Holland Park Avenue, Holland Park

The BBC used a large house in Holland Park Avenue for the pilot episode of the comedy *You Rang M'Lord?* – but after that Lord Meldrum's house was a fake.

For later episodes the show's production team re-created the down-stairs exterior of the house on location in Norfolk and also in a car park at the BBC's Elstree Studios. 'We had to build the set and hope it wouldn't rain,' says Director Roy Gould.

Subsequently, privately-owned Bayfield Hall, Bayfield, Norfolk became Sir Ralph Shawcross' country house, and the grounds were used to film various other scenes as well as doubling as the grounds of Lord Meldrum's house.

The church used for the wedding in the last series was St Mary's Church in Sporle near Swaffham, and the final shots of the last-ever episode were shot on the beach at Cromer, 300 yards away from the pier.

EASTENDERS

BBC Studios, Elstree

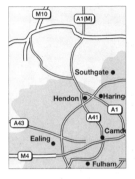

Like *The Bill* and *Brookside, EastEnders* is a problem for location fans because there is nothing for them to see. *EastEnders* is shot almost entirely on a specially built set at a BBC Studio in North London.

The Albert Square set we see on screen was based on real life Fassett Square in Hackney and although it looks real on screen it is actually constructed from fibreglass and plasterboard. 'The construction of the set took place between May and November 1984,' explains Designer Keith Harris. 'We were very lucky, the weather was beautiful every day and so we finished on time. My only worry was that the set wouldn't have time to weather – it needed the dust to settle on it and to be washed with the rain, frost and snow. I think it's just coming on now – more than ten years later!

'At one time I didn't think the Square would last three years, let alone more than ten. After the hurricane of October 1987 I came to check the set with a feeling of impending doom. The roads were blocked with the fallen trees and when I got to Elstree the security guards told me the damage was pretty bad. Expecting the worst, I approached the set to discover that luckily it was virtually untouched by the violent storms – the security guards had been having me on!'

Left: The Mitchell family, Phil, Grant and mum Peggy.

Above: Martin Kemp, who terrorised Albert Square as the murderous Steve.

The houses actually have no backs as the interior shots
are filmed at an adjacent studio. When the set was first built
it had just three sides and Bridge Street, but over the years
various buildings have been added, including Frank and
Pat's B&B, Michelle's flat and Frank's car lot, as well as
George Street, Turpin Road, a chippie, a betting shop and a
row of houses. Recently more people have moved into

George Street and Guiseppe's restaurant has been added to
Albert Square.

Because *EastEnders* has a working set, the BBC can't
accommodate visitors. But *EastEnders* fans can visit various
locations used on the programme which aren't inside
Elstree Studios. For example, Den Watts was shot by the
side of the Grand Union Canal, near Water Road, London

NW10; Lofty and Michelle's marriage was filmed at the chapel in the grounds of Shenley Hospital, Shenley in Hertfordshire; and Charlie Cotton's funeral, which coincided with the blessing of Ricky and Sam's marriage, was filmed at St Nicholas' Church, Elstree Hill, Elstree.

But you won't find the resting place of Lou Beale or Ali and Sue's baby – scenes where families visit their relatives' graves are shot on a grassy patch outside the *EastEnders* production offices at Elstree. More recently we have seen *EastEnders* going to Europe – Paris, Italy, Spain – and travelling closer to home – Blackpool, Devon, the Norfolk Broads and Ireland.

GOODNIGHT SWEETHEART

Bethnal Green

The BBC comedy series *Goodnight Sweetheart* stars Nicholas Lyndhurst as Gary Sparrow, the man who lives between two different time zones, one modern day and the other during the Second World War.

Unlike in *Doctor Who*, we never see how Gary manages to travel in time: he simply walks down a passageway off a London street and switches time. The passageway, Ducketts Passage, is actually Ezra Street near the flower market off Columbia Road, Bethnal Green.

His 1940s wife Phoebe, played by Liz Carling, runs a pub, The Royal Oak, and that is played by the real-life Royal Oak in Columbia Road. It's no stranger to the screen, and has also been used for the film *Lock, Stock and Two Smoking Barrels* and the BBC series *The Hello Girls*.

When the *Goodnight Sweetheart* team arrived, they altered the pub by putting sandbags by the door and by putting tape on the windows, as was recommended during the Blitz to stop flying glass in the event of a bomb. They also parked contemporary vehicles in the street nearby. They used rooms upstairs in the pub as green rooms where actors wait until needed for filming and the staff enjoyed having them there. 'They filmed up to the door and then it cut to the studio,' explains publican Mervyn Miller. 'The pub was built in 1924, but they thought that the interior was a bit too modern to play 1940s. It was great to have them filming at the pub and we enjoyed them being here. A few locals remembered what the pub was like in the war and they thought it was fabulous.'

The exterior of Gary's wartime memorabilia shop Blitz and Pieces was in nearby Old Street and the interior was a studio set. For the 1999 series, the sixth, the locations weren't used and instead were re-created at Shepperton Studios, Surrey.

MINDER

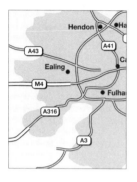

Even Arthur Daley was conned every time he went into the Winchester Club – because it was actually a studio set. But that wasn't always the way. In some early episodes of the popular ITV series about the exploits of dodgy-dealing Arthur Daley, a drinking club in Chalk Farm, north London, situated next to the tube station, was used.

Glynn Edwards, who played Winchester Club barman Dave, recalled: 'We took over the whole place and used inside and outside, but that was short-lived because it didn't work out from the producer's point of view, and so after that we used sets in a studio.'

The outside door to the Winchester Club actually belonged to a building at 2b Newburgh Road, Acton, West London – but characters were never actually seen going through it because it led into a private flat. Over the years the exterior location of the Winchester Club has changed around six times. All the production team did was find a suitable property and then put up the Club's sign and a canopy.

Arthur's car lot has changed location over the years, but the one last used by the *Minder* production team was at 89 Churchfield Road, Acton. 'It was an empty site and we took a lease out on it when we filmed,' explained a member of the production team. 'We did this because we needed full control of the site for six months, and if we used someone else's place and, after a few months, they got fed up and didn't want you back, then the game would be up for continuity. So we preferred to play it safe and take the whole site lock, stock and barrel.'

Previously real car lots had been used, but for the last series the *Minder* props team dressed the site with cars and added Arthur's office and the Daley Motors signs. Similarly, Arthur's lock-up, where he kept all his dodgy gear, had changed since *Minder* began. For the last series it was at the rear of 7 Standard Road, Park Royal, in West London. Before filming began the *Minder* props team filled the lock-up with the boxes and junk which played Arthur's merchandise. We never saw where Arthur's home was, but the exterior of Ray Daley's flat was at 33b Alfred Road, Acton.

Arthur was always trying to keep one step ahead of the law and, as with the other locations used in *Minder*, the police station in the series changed regularly. For later series it was The Priory Centre, a community centre in Petersfield Road. And as for the pier that Arthur and Ray were always seen walking down during *Minder*'s title sequence – that is Southend Pier in Essex.

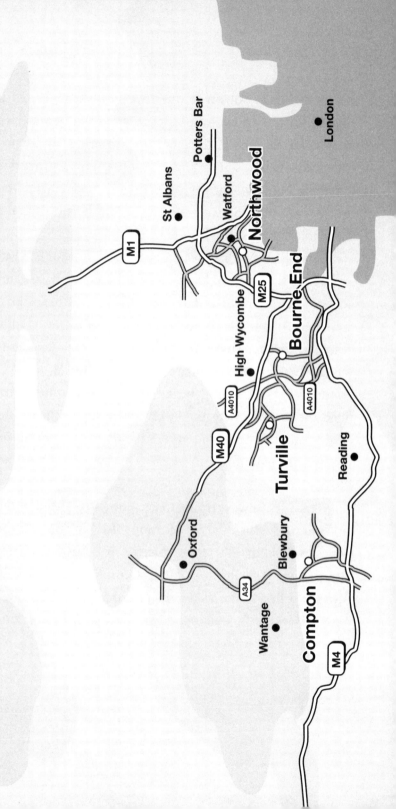

THE HOME COUNTIES

TRAINER

Trainer galloped onto our screens in 1991, a story of passion and rivalry in the world of horse racing. The BBC hoped the series would be as popular as its highly successful sailing and sex drama *Howard's Way*, but after two series they decided to put it out to grass.

The series was set at Arkenfield Stables at Arkenfield, which in reality were Hamilton Stables at Compton on the Berkshire Downs near Newbury, owned by real-life trainer Peter Cundell. The BBC changed the signs, moved in its own horses, and hired actors to wander round in jodhpurs.

The nearby 19th century manor house, Roden House, real-life home to Peter and his wife Maureen, also featured in the series as the Ware Stud, house of Rachel Ware, played by Susannah York.

The show's main characters, which included Mark Greenstreet as moody trainer Mike Hardy and David McCallum as gambling expert John Grey, would often be seen at their local pub, The Dog and Gun, which was actually The Crown and Horn at nearby East Ilsley. Racecourse scenes for *Trainer* were filmed on actual race days at several courses including Bath, Goodwood, and Newbury.

PORRIDGE

The Gate House, 152 Victoria Street, St Albans, Hertfordshire

You wouldn't have found inmates if you took a look behind the gates of HM Prison Slade on the classic television comedy series *Porridge* – but you would have found row upon row of council dustcarts. The front of Britain's most famous prison – where Norman Stanley Fletcher did his porridge – was actually filmed at a council depot at St Albans in Hertfordshire. BBC designers put up the HM Prison Slade signs, barred nearby windows and built a set of double doors at the end of the gatehouse entrance tunnel.

The real Victorian St Albans Prison, which had room for 85 men and 14 women in separate cells, and saw four executions, the last one being in 1914, became a military detention barracks in 1915 and was used by the army until 1919. It then stood empty for ten years before it was bought by St Albans City Council in 1930 as a depot for their Highways Department. Recently it has become the sales and marketing headquarters of mineral water company, Highland Spring.

The BBC used the gatehouse as the front of Slade Prison after the Home Office refused to allow them to film *Porridge* at an actual prison. 'When the series started they let the writers, Dick Clement and Ian La Frenais, go in to a prison for research, but they were very sticky about letting myself and the designer in,' recalls Producer Sydney Lotterby.

'We were forever saying: "Can we get in? It's all right for the authors because they've written the stuff, but we need to see what it's like." So it wasn't until the third series that they let me go into Lewes Jail.' The visit was worthwhile and helped Sydney with background information, like the fact that prisoners used to split a single match into two or three to make a box last longer. He was later able to incorporate that sort of detail into a scene.

The exterior scenes inside Slade Prison were filmed at various mental institutions around the outskirts of London. Sydney explains: 'The windows of these places used to be very small with tiny panes of glass and from a distance they actually looked like prison bars so that's why we filmed there.'

The interior scenes inside Slade were filmed in a BBC studio. One scene required a three-storey set complete with prison-type netting, so designers built a replica prison wing in a tank at Ealing film studios. The water was let out, then the ground floor of the wing was built at the bottom, the first floor, on the ground level, and then the second floor on top of that with scaffolding. 'It cost a lot of money but was quite incredible,' recalls Sydney. 'It looked spectacular.'

The Home Office has relaxed its bar on filming in prisons since *Porridge* began in 1974, and now allows television companies to film in prisons for a fee. There is usually a long waiting list, as they only allow closed wings to be used, usually before or after they are refurbished. Obviously security is tight. Film crews and their equipment are always searched and the wings they are using for filming are always securely shut off from other parts of the prison.

THE VICAR OF DIBLEY

Turville, Buckinghamshire

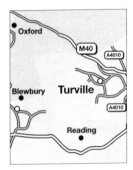

The gentle BBC comedy series *The Vicar of Dibley*, which stars Dawn French as local vicar Reverend Geraldine Granger, is filmed in the Buckinghamshire village of Turville with the local church St Mary the Virgin doubling as fictional St Barnabus Church.

The exterior for the screen vicarage is actually two cottages in the village which are made to look like one house, but interior shots are filmed weeks later at the BBC studios in London, with a fake backdrop in place at the front door for continuity.

Turville is no stranger to film crews as a nearby windmill was used for the classic 1968 film *Chitty Chitty Bang Bang*, which starred Dick Van Dyke and Sally Ann Howes, and for the 1996 live action version of *101 Dalmatians*. More recently it was used as the village of Weirfold for the ITV wartime drama *Goodnight Mister Tom* which starred John Thaw as widowed and cantankerous Tom Oakley whose life is changed when nine-year-old Willie Beech is billeted with him.

Right: St Mary the Virgin Church at Turville, location for the *Vicar of Dibley*.

FAWLTY TOWERS

Wooburn Grange, Bourne End, Buckinghamshire

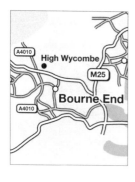

Sadly the real house used on-screen as the infamous Fawlty Towers hotel was bulldozed in early 1993. Wooburn Grange, at Bourne End in Buckinghamshire, was ravaged by fire in March 1991 just before it was due to be renovated and was hit by a second blaze just four months later.

The building played an important role in the classic seventies BBC comedy which starred John Cleese as manic hotel boss Basil Fawlty, Prunella Scales as his domineering wife Sybil, Connie Booth as waitress Polly and Andrew Sachs as Manuel, the Spanish waiter.

Fawlty Towers hotel was supposed to be in Torquay, Devon but BBC bosses chose the Buckinghamshire site because it was more convenient to London. After filming ended, Wooburn Grange became a nightclub called Basil's, and was later used as an Indian restaurant. By the spring of 1993 it had vanished completely and had been replaced by eight five-bedroom family homes.

THE GOOD LIFE

Kewferry Road, Northwood, Middlesex

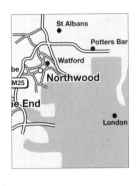

The classic seventies comedy *The Good Life* saw Tom and Barbara Good turn their middle-class home in Surbiton into a self-sufficient empire of vegetables and animals. Thousands copied their idea, and countless lawns all over the country were dug up and replaced by rows of carrots and turnips. Tom and Barbara's lifestyle, however, was far from ideal for their upmarket next-door neighbours Margo and Gerry Leadbetter, played by Penelope Keith and Paul Eddington, who awoke each morning to the sound of pigs and hens.

In the series Kewferry Road in Northwood, Middlesex doubled for the fictional road, The Avenue, in Surbiton, Surrey, because it was easier for the crew and actors to travel from BBC Television Centre to Northwood with their cameras and props than Surbiton.

Finding two suitable houses side by side for the series, one slightly run-down and one immaculate could have been a problem but location managers struck lucky in Kewferry Road.

'They were very lucky,' recalls Richard Briers. 'Tom and Barbara's house was 1930s and a bit peeling and a little bit shabby, and Gerry and Margo's was one of those Hendon-type houses, very smart with bay windows and with a much smarter garden so we didn't have to do anything to it, which was very lucky.'

Of course, the then owners of the Goods' house, number 55, had agreed to have both their fully-lawned front and back gardens dug up and covered with vegetables, not to mention having animals running round – and one of their rooms doubled as a make-up and costume store.

After each series, a BBC crew dug up the vegetables and re-laid the turf – and after the final series the production team even added a patio for them.

Playing host to *The Good Life* film crew wasn't always easy though. For one episode the fire brigade stood in the front garden spraying their hoses over the roof into the back garden as rain – turning the back garden into something resembling the Somme. But allowing their home to star in the series, which ran for four series over ten years from 1975, did have its compensations when it came to moving, as the fact that the house had played host to *The Good Life* team was a valuable selling point.

Richard adds: 'The people we rented it from moved out when the series finished for good and, of course, got more money for it, because it was the famous *Good Life* house, so they did very well out of it!'

DOCTOR WHO

Home Counties

In the 30 years since *Doctor Who* began, the time-travelling Doctor has been all over the galaxy – without leaving Earth! Credit must go to the show's many location managers who, over the years, have managed to find dozens of British locations to play either far-off planets or Earth in the past, present or future. What follows are some of the more interesting locations used over the years for filming *Doctor Who* – but clearly it is not an exhaustive list. See the further reading list for details of specific *Doctor Who* publications that include further information on locations.

THE FIRST DOCTOR –
William Hartnell (1963-1966)

Back in 1964, when the late William Hartnell played the Doctor, the dreaded Daleks invaded the planet in the story 'The Dalek Invasion of Earth' and were seen roaming in London near the Houses of Parliament, in Trafalgar Square, on Westminster Bridge, on the South Bank, at Whitehall, and at the Albert Memorial in the first real location sequences using dialogue.

The footage shot in Trafalgar Square was shot at 5am and was supposed to show deserted London where everyone was hiding away from the Daleks. And it certainly looked deserted – except that if you look very carefully you will see a bus!

THE SECOND DOCTOR –
Patrick Troughton (1966-1969)

Doctor number two, played by the late Patrick Troughton, landed his TARDIS at Gatwick Airport in the story 'The Faceless Ones', and spent time at Sennen, Helson and Porthcurno in Cornwall for the 1966 adventure 'The Smugglers'.

The Nant Ffrancon Pass and Ogwen Lake in Snowdonia, Wales, played a more exotic location: Tibet, home of the Yeti – or so it appeared, in the 1967 story 'The Abominable Snowman'. But when the Yeti took over the London underground in 'The Web of Fear', London Transport demanded so high a fee for the use of its tube tunnels – and then only in the early hours of the morning – that the BBC filmed most of the series on studio sets.

The series took to the sea – in actuality, the Thames Estuary – for the 1968 story 'Fury From The Deep', filming on the Radio 390 Offshore Platform at Red Sands and, when back on land, on the beach at Margate in Kent.

One of the series' most visually spectacular location sequences came in the 1968 story 'The Invasion' where a supposedly massive invasion of Cybermen swept London. After emerging from sewers, the Cybermen were later seen descending St Paul's Cathedral steps, in scenes which must have made thousands of children hide behind the sofa.

THE THIRD DOCTOR –

Jon Pertwee (1970-1974)

When Jon Pertwee took over the role of the Doctor in 1970 he came face to face in his first adventure with plastic monsters, the Autons, in 'Spearhead from Space'. In another eerie sequence, the Autons, in the guise of tailors' dummies, came alive in a shop window, smashed their way out and started walking down the street shooting people. This scene was filmed early one Sunday morning at Ealing Broadway in West London. The inside of Madame Tussaud's in London was also used for a scene.

The story also called for scenes at a hospital and at the headquarters of the United Nations Intelligence Task Force (UNIT) – and these were shot at the BBC's Engineering Training Centre at Wood Norton, near Evesham.

In the 1971 story 'The Mind of Evil', Dover Castle played a prison where the evil Master, played by Roger Delgado, was being kept under lock and key. During the story prisoners took over the prison and the authorities sent in UNIT troops to storm it in one of the programme's finest action sequences.

Later that year the Wiltshire village of Aldbourne

played the fictional village of Devil's End in the popular story 'The Daemons'. The village pub, The Blue Boar, doubled as The Cloven Hoof and the village church was used as the church which was seen exploding in the final episode. This scene caused complaints from some viewers who thought the BBC had destroyed a real church. The church which was blown up was, of course, just a cleverly-made model. The barrow, which played Devil's Hump in the series, is about ¼ of a mile from Aldbourne up a dirt track.

The 1972 story 'The Sea Devils' used one of the most unusual locations – a 19th century fort in the sea between Portsmouth and the Isle of Wight. The No Man's Land fort, one of four in the sea, was built to keep the French out. Once owned by the MOD, it has now been turned into a luxury home and was recently on the market for £950,000 – down from the £6 million asking price during the 80s property boom.

The Royal Navy helped the BBC with 'The Sea Devils' and allowed them to use its Whale Island base, *HMS Excellent*, in Portsmouth as the fictional *HMS Seaspite* in the story and also the nearby Frazer Gunnery Range. This time Norris Castle on the Isle of Wight was used as a prison for the dastardly villain, The Master.

In the 1973 story 'The Three Doctors', a large house in Haylings Lane, Denham in Buckinghamshire became UNIT headquarters and some footage of William Hartnell, who was too ill to film in London, was recorded in the garden of his home in Mayfield, Sussex.

THE FOURTH DOCTOR –
Tom Baker (1975-1981)

During Tom Baker's first series as the Doctor, the caves at Wookey Hole at Wells in Somerset were used for 'The Revenge of the Cybermen'. Scotland was the setting for the first story of Baker's second season but the BBC decided against going north and instead travelled to locations near Bognor Regis in West Sussex to film 'The Terror of The Zygons'. Using carefully selected locations – not to mention music with a clear Scottish flavour – it actually worked pretty well and certainly saved the BBC a large amount of money. The pub used in the story is The Fox Goes Free at Charlton in West Sussex.

Athelhampton House, near Dorchester in Dorset, was the location for the 1976 adventure 'The Seeds of Doom', and it is open to the public. It wasn't the first time Athelhampton had been used by film crews: Michael Caine and Laurence Olivier filmed *Sleuth* there in 1972.

Mick Jagger's former home, Stargroves, at Pangbourne in Berkshire was used in stories 'The Pyramids of Mars' and 'The Image of The Fendahl', and Dartmoor was the location for the story 'The Sontaran Experiment'.

THE FIFTH DOCTOR –
Peter Davison (1982-1984)

Peter Davison, the fifth Doctor, filmed some of the period story 'The Visitation at Black Park' near Pinewood, and some of 'Time-Flight' at Heathrow Airport. Davison's story 'Mawdryn Undead' was filmed at Middlesex Polytechnic, Trent Park, Barnet.

Much of the 1984 story 'The Resurrection of The Daleks' was filmed in London's Docklands on Shad Thames, a road that ran through lots of old factories on the south side of the River Thames which have all been renovated. The actual warehouse used is now a restaurant called Le Pont de la Tour.

THE SIXTH DOCTOR –
Colin Baker (1984-1986)

Sixth Doctor Colin Baker had to endure freezing

temperatures when he filmed his only Dalek story, 'Revelation of the Daleks', in the snow at Butser Hill near Petersfield, Hampshire. IBM's futuristic UK head-quarters at North Harbour, Portsmouth, was used for later scenes also shot in the snow, when a statue crushes the Doctor.

During the 'Mindwarp' story some scenes were filmed on the nudist section of Brighton beach, and they had to make sure they kept the nude bathers out of shot.

THE SEVENTH DOCTOR –

Sylvester McCoy (1987-1989)

Seventh Doctor Sylvester McCoy was supposed to film his 1988 story 'Silver Nemesis' at Windsor Castle, but this was blocked by officials so the shoot was switched to Arundel Castle in West Sussex which played Windsor instead. The picturesque town around the stunning castle, which is open to visitors, was also used for filming. In later scenes Greenwich Gas Works was used as a landing site for a Cyberfleet.

THE EIGHTH DOCTOR –

Paul McGann (1996)

Paul McGann has so far made just one appearance as the Eighth Doctor in the 1996 adventure 'Enemy Within' which was filmed in Canada and San Francisco.

Much of the 20th Anniversary show, 'The Five Doctors', was filmed in North Wales, although one of Jon Pertwee's sequences in his car, Bessie, was filmed in Denham.

The footage of Tom Baker, who was unavailable to take part in the programme, was taken from the 1979 story 'Shada', which was never completed because of a BBC strike. In the sequences, the Doctor and his assistant Romana, played by Lalla Ward, are seen punting on the river in Cambridge.

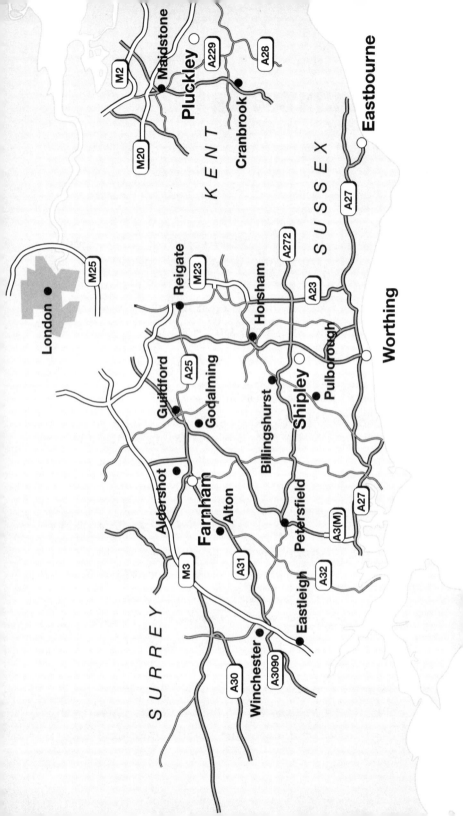

THE SOUTH EAST

WESTBEACH

When the BBC drama *Westbeach* began, there was criticism from some local people that the programme made the town of Eastbourne look dreary. Yet others claimed that the publicity the series brought the seaside town could only help to attract more visitors. Whatever the truth, Eastbourne has always been a popular choice for sunseekers young and old, and probably always will be. The drama focused on the rival Preston and Cromer families both vying for the

The 'Royal Suffolk' Hotel that confused holiday makers!

biggest share of business in the fictional south coast resort of Westbeach.

Former *Bergerac* star Deborah Grant played tough Sarah Preston who ran the family hotel The Royal Suffolk. The Queen's Hotel played The Royal Suffolk in the series and was actually part of the De Vere chain. The BBC decided only to use the hotel for exterior shots and re-created the inside of the hotel, including the bar and reception area, at a recently closed girls' school.

But even just using the outside of the hotel caused confusion when residents returning from a walk along the promenade found that the exterior signs had been changed to those of the fictitious Royal Suffolk Hotel.

Westbeach Producer Susi Hush says: 'They looked very bewildered when they came back to find their hotel had changed names. Some of them even wandered off to look for the original Queen's Hotel somewhere else, as if they'd got lost.'

IT AIN'T HALF HOT MUM

Farnham, Surrey

You could be mistaken for thinking that the BBC comedy *It Ain't Half Hot Mum*, which was set in wartime Burma, was actually filmed in a hot, sticky climate. But that was just clever make-up. The series, featuring the exploits of an army concert party, was actually filmed at BBC studios and the furthest location used were woods at Farnham in Surrey.

And, as with *Dad's Army*, the MOD allowed the BBC to film on its land, this time in woodlands. Clever set-dressing turned Farnham into Burma. Writer Jimmy Perry recalls: 'We used to put rubber palms and rubber jungle creepers in the ground.'

Actor Ken MacDonald was thrilled when he was given the part of banjo-playing Gunner Clark, particularly at the thought of filming in some exotic foreign location. 'We ended up in these woods in Farnham,' he laughs. 'But it was a great show to get into and tremendous fun.'

And although Michael Knowles, who played dashing Captain Ashwood, loved working on the show, he doesn't miss the daily routine he faced on the set of *It Ain't Half Hot Mum* – being covered in fake sweat. 'It was agony,' he recalls. 'We always filmed around October and had a lot of lighting to make it look hot and they used to spray this glycerine and water stuff on us. And the sand would blow up and stick on you and then it would trickle into your mouth. As soon as we dried out under the lights they sprayed more on us!'

MEN BEHAVING BADLY

Worthing, West Sussex

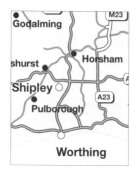

The town of Worthing in West Sussex featured heavily in the second episode of the final trilogy of the hilarious BBC comedy *Men Behaving Badly*, broadcast over three nights during Christmas 1998. The story saw Gary, played by Martin Clunes, attending a security equipment conference in the town and his girlfriend Dorothy (Caroline Quentin), pal Tony (Neil Morrissey) and his girlfriend Deborah (Leslie Ash) decide to come too.

They stay at the aptly named Groyne View Hotel in Worthing, which isn't the most romantic venue for a seaside break, especially when all four of them are sharing one room with peeling wallpaper.

And while Tony, Dorothy and Deborah entertain themselves during the day with crazy golf, Gary becomes preoccupied with an attractive female delegate at the conference. Tony and Deborah step in to save Gary and

Dorothy's relationship, and the crazy golf course comes off worst.

In real life, the building used as the Groyne View Hotel isn't a hotel at all but is actually Crown Agents International Management Training Centre, 3-10 Marine Parade. The company, which specialises in training overseas civil servants, let the BBC use the outside of the building and the lounge and bar area for the conference scene. It was a perfect setting as the building used to be a three-star hotel.

The pier was also used, as was the beach just to the east of the pier where Tony and Gary got drunk in a mock-up car. Flash Point, at the end of the promenade, was also used for the crazy golf course where Gary and Tony had a fight. The course doesn't really exist and was all built by the BBC props team. 'I'm sure that next summer thousands of people are going to ask us where the crazy golf is,' says Foreshore Manager Mike Colliss. 'And the truth is that Worthing doesn't have one at all!' For more information about Worthing contact the Tourist Information Centre on (01903) 210022.

JONATHAN CREEK

Shipley, Sussex

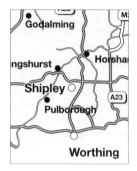

Jonathan Creek isn't your average television detective and it's therefore quite apt that he doesn't have a typical home. In fact, Jonathan's home couldn't really be more unusual. After all, how many other television characters live in a windmill?

In David Renwick's cleverly crafted mystery series *Jonathan Creek*, the eponymous hero, played by Alan Davies, and his investigative crime writer colleague Maddy Magellan, played by Caroline Quentin, solve seemingly impossible crimes. Jonathan's real job is devising magic tricks and illusions for flamboyant illusionist Adam Klaus and it's his probing, lateral mind and ability to think round corners that makes him a key player in Maddy's quest for the truth.

The real-life windmill used in *Jonathan Creek* has an interesting history of its own. It is actually Shipley Windmill in the pretty West Sussex village of the same name and was once owned by the renowned writer and MP Hilaire Belloc. There's a plaque to him on the side of the windmill that reads: 'Let this be a memorial to Hilaire Belloc who garnered a harvest of wisdom and sympathy for young and old.'

Despite its looks, it's actually the youngest – and the

largest – windmill in Sussex, having been built in 1879 for a Mr Frend Marten by Horsham millwrights Grist and Steele. It cost £2,500, some £1,700 more than originally estimated.

In 1906 the mill, nearby Kings Land house and the surrounding land were bought by Hilaire Belloc. With the advent of freely available electricity and motor vehicles, windmills across Britain began to be used less often as they became uneconomic to run. Shipley Mill, however, combatted this for a while by having a steam engine fitted that so it could be used on days when there was no wind, and the mill continued to be used until the end of its active life in 1926.

Finally, big roller mills put windmills like Shipley out of business. Between the wars Hilaire Belloc tried to keep the windmill in good order, but the shortage of materials during the Second World War meant that by the time of Belloc's death in 1953 it needed considerable work to halt its decline. An appeal was launched to restore the mill as a memorial to Hilaire Belloc, and a local committee was formed and gained the support of the West Sussex County Council; the mill was reopened in 1958.

In 1986, major repairs were again needed and a charitable Trust was formed consisting of various council representatives: the Friends of Shipley Windmill, the Society for the Protection of Ancient Buildings, the Book Trust and Charles Eustace, Belloc's great grandson, who has given the Trust a 20-year lease at a peppercorn rent. In 1990 the mill was re-opened, with just a single pair of sweeps, but a year later a second pair were added, restoring the mill to its former glory.

You won't find any permanent reminders of *Jonathan Creek,* because all Jonathan's artefacts are brought down for filming by the BBC's design team.

'The BBC investigated using a few mills across the South and decided that Shipley Windmill was the right one,' says Gillian French of the Friends of Shipley Windmill. 'They keep it very low key when they film here, and they don't disturb anyone. The production team film both inside and out, so when they arrive they move out the usual contents and then fill it with all their props to make it look like Jonathan Creek's home. It's quite a transformation.'

The mill continues to be open to the public on the first and third Sundays in the month from Easter to October, Bank Holiday Mondays, and on National Mills Day from 2-5pm. 1999 prices were £1.50 for adults, 50p for children and concessions are £1. Flour milled on-site is sometimes available for purchase.

The next project for the Friends of the Shipley Windmill is to rebuild the engine shed on the side of the windmill and buy a diesel engine so they can mill on the days when there is no wind. 'We've got an English Heritage grant for a percentage of the cost, but we've still got to raise thousands more,' says Gillian French.

Left: Alan Davies and Caroline Quentin take a break during the filming of *Jonathan Creek* at Shipley Windmill.

Inset: The Shipley Windmill.

THE DARLING BUDS OF MAY

Pluckley, Kent

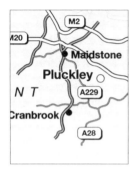

The sleepy village of Pluckley in Kent had never expected the attention that it suddenly received in the summer of 1991. For the instant success of Yorkshire Television's *The Darling Buds Of May*, starring the ever-popular David Jason as Pop Larkin, brought hordes of fans into the village, which is said to be one of the most haunted places in Britain.

The quaint, 15th century Black Horse pub plays the Hare and Hound in the series and has been a great attraction to visitors. When the series began, though, the pub did not manage to catch the first fans because it was closed for redecoration. 'We still get people coming to the village because of *The Darling Buds of May* and it's still good for business,' says landlady Patricia McLaren. 'And they also come here for the ghosts.'

Just across the road is Robin Smith's grocer's shop, which featured in the series. Next door to it is George Holmewood's butcher's shop. 'This shop was here when H E Bates wrote the stories,' says George. 'My father ran it then.'

St Nicholas Parish Church became a star attraction of the series when Mariette, played by Catherine Zeta Jones, married Charley (Philip Franks). And it was also used when Primrose Larkin (Abigail Rokinson) was chasing the Reverend Candy, played by Tyler Butterworth. Next door to the church is the house that played guide mistress Edith Pilchester's home and opposite the church is the cottage, which played Orchard Cottage where the Brigadier, played by Moray Watson, lived. A few doors away is the local school which was used in the series as the village hall.

A few miles away from Pluckley, on the road to Smarden, is Bliss Farm, which played the Larkin's Home Farm. When the series first began, dozens of fans arrived wanting to look round the farm. But visitors aren't welcome, as the sign at the farm's entrance makes clear, and the farm cannot be seen from the road. Owner Raymond Holmes had spent years making the five-bedroom farmhouse look modern and then the *Darling Buds Of May* crew arrived – and made it look old again to fit the fifties feel of the programme.

The Darling Buds of May production team stumbled on the farm after spending two weeks looking for the ideal location. 'It was quite difficult to find something that fitted the bill,' explained Production Designer Alan Davis. 'The problem was that many of the houses had been renovated and dolled up.'

The farmhouse still had to be repainted before filming began – and white again afterwards. A modern extension at the back of the house was out of keeping with the fifties period. Alan soon devised a plan to disguise it. 'We decided to cover the whole thing in Kentish weatherboarding to make

it look a bit more rural and in keeping with the local architecture,' he says. It worked and the extension is used in the show as the Larkins' billiard room.

One thing Alan didn't want in the series was a modern greenhouse in the garden. As ever, he found a solution. 'We built an old shed to put in front of the greenhouse and block it out of sight,' he reveals. The summerhouse is a bit of a cheat, although you won't see it as such in the programme. It is actually just three sided!

Next job was to add ivy and dead vine to the house. 'We put ivy on to take the edge off the squareness of the place,' says Alan. The dead vine goes on first and then silk and plastic ivy – all bought by the sackload – is stapled on branch by branch. Alan prefers the plastic. He says: 'It tends to look more realistic on camera than the silk. It really blends in.'

The farmyard was Alan's biggest headache. It needed to be filled with 1950s junk. So Alan and the show's prop buyer roamed the Kent countryside with a heavy lifting vehicle in convoy hunting for junk! They snapped up everything that Pop Larkin would have littering his farmyard. 'We got whatever we could find,' says Alan. 'We picked up tons of apple boxes, an old tractor, an old conveyor, apple-picking ladders, barrels, general scrap metal, lots of oil drums, tyres, an old pitch boiling tank, an old water tank and any farm machinery we saw.'

As the junk was strewn across the farmyard Alan kept his eye out for something that would be out of keeping with the fifties feel of the show, namely plastic. 'When things are rusty they just blend in,' he explains. 'But we had to be careful about the odd bit of plastic.' More vine and ivy was added in amongst the junk to make it look more established.

The house's original studded oak front and back door were also replaced with fake fifties panel and glazed doors to match the studio set.

Everything was very nearly perfick. But one problem had gone unsolved – and Alan was stumped. Nettles! Not too many of them, but too few. Alan explains: 'In the book there are references to lots of nettles in amongst the scrap and junk but if there's one thing you can't transplant it is weeds!'

'You can't actually dig up some nettles or thistles and put them in a pot and water them and expect them to grow because they never do,' he says. 'There's something about weeds that they just don't like being moved.'

So the team just had to make do with a bit more of the good old dead vine. And by the end, the whole place looked just perfick! Some scenes in later episodes of *The Darling Buds Of May*, supposed to be set in Kent, were actually filmed hundreds of miles away in Yorkshire – to save time and money. 'It's a question of cost,' explains David Jason. 'The producers found that they could get locations in Leeds that looked like Kent. That way they could save money because they didn't have to ship the crew all the way down to Kent and pay for hotels there. As long as it looks like Kent and can convince us all then that's fine. They are very careful to make sure no one can say: "That can never be Kent."'

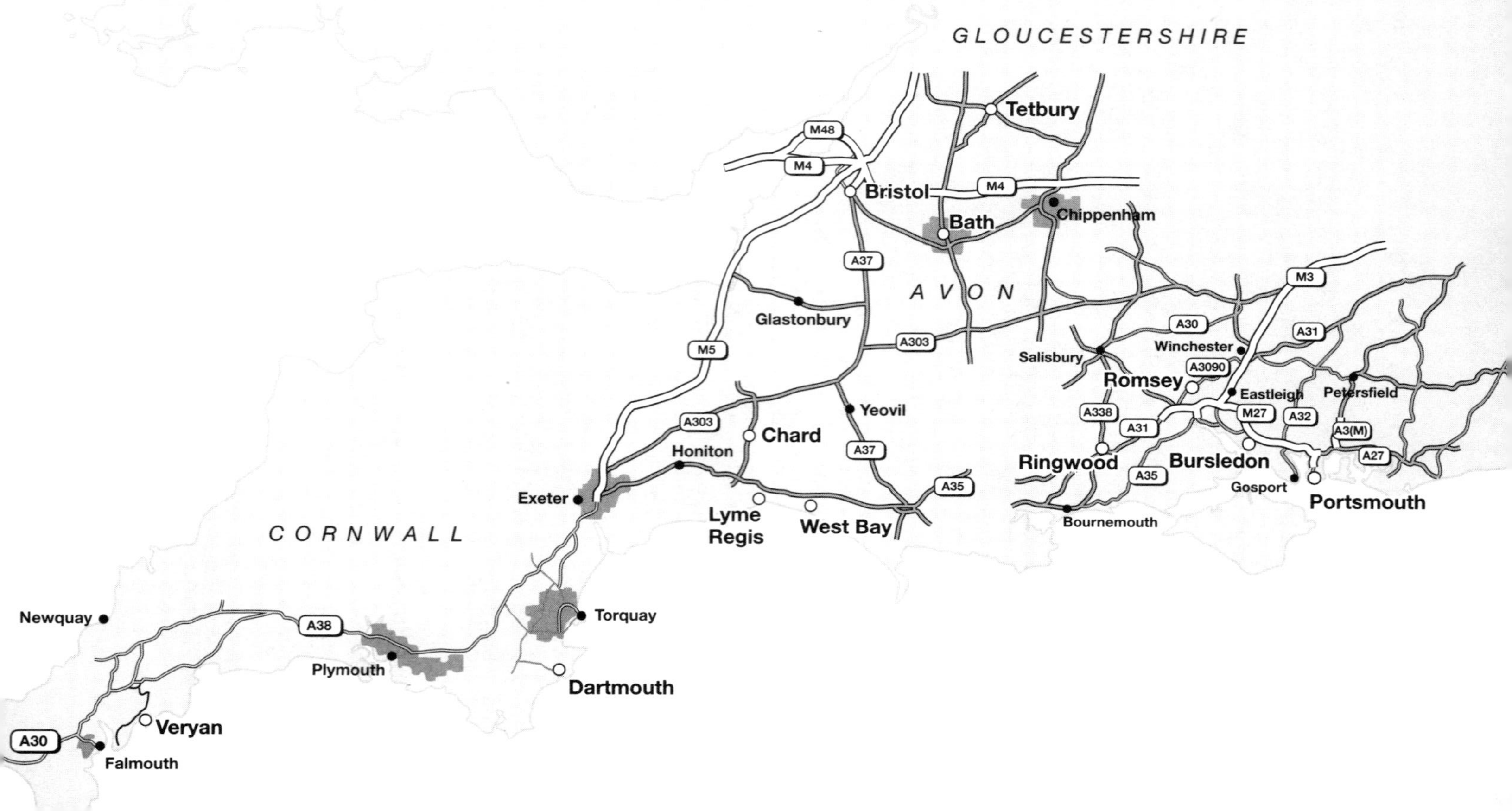
GLOUCESTERSHIRE
Tetbury
M48
M4
Bristol
M4
Bath
Chippenham
A37
AVON
M3
Glastonbury
A30
A31
M5
A303
Winchester
Salisbury
A3090
Romsey
Eastleigh
Petersfield
Yeovil
A338
M27
A32
A303
A31
A3(M)
Chard
A37
Honiton
Ringwood
Bursledon
A27
A35
A35
Gosport
Exeter
Portsmouth
Lyme Regis
West Bay
Bournemouth
CORNWALL
Newquay
Torquay
A38
Plymouth
Dartmouth
Veryan
A30
Falmouth

THE SOUTH WEST

WYCLIFFE

Cornwall

In terms of stunning locations, the ITV detective drama *Wycliffe* was the best television advertisement for the county of Cornwall since *Poldark* was a huge hit for the BBC back in the seventies.

Jack Shepherd starred as likeable Cornish sleuth Detective Superintendent Charles Wycliffe alongside his faithful team of Jimmy Yuill and Helen Masters as Detective Inspectors Doug Kersey and Lucy Lane.

Together they solved all manner of baffling cases during the show's five series which ran from a pilot episode in 1993 until 1998. The production base was Truro, but locations all over Cornwall from quiet farmhouses and pretty fishing villages to cliffs buffeted by raging seas and upmarket houses were used for filming of the series.

'Get a map and stick a pin in at Truro and draw a 30 mile radius from it and you're bound to come across a *Wycliffe* location,' said a member of the production team. 'We used hundreds of different places for filming over the length of the series. We were given great co-operation by local authorities, the tourist bodies and residents. They were marvellous and we couldn't have made the series without them.'

The dramatic scene in the opening episode, when a man out walking his dog is gunned down, was filmed at Caerhays beach below Caerhays Castle, and in another episode a burning wheel was pushed off a stunning peak, actually the National Trust-owned Pentire Point, a beauty spot much loved by walkers.

The Wild West theme park featured in the episode 'The Scapegoat' was actually Frontier City near St Columb Major, and the whole village of St Ewe was taken over by the film crew for the episode 'The Last Rites'.

Other key scenes were filmed at Porthleven, Redruth, Portreath, Goonhilly Down, the BT communications centre in Carharrach and Kennach Sands. The shot of an exploding fishing boat in the episode 'The Pea Green Boat' was filmed off Godrevy Point near Hayle, and a car going off a cliff in the same episode was filmed at Porthowan.

ONLY FOOLS AND HORSES

Bristol, Brighton, Salisbury, Ipswich, Hull and London

It's no real wonder that the long arms of the law have never quite managed to catch up with dodgy-dealing Del Boy Trotter. For if the boys in blue have been looking for Del in his manor of Peckham, they've been looking in the wrong place.

Only Fools And Horses, which stars David Jason as wheeler-dealer Del Boy and Nicholas Lyndhurst as his dopey brother Rodney, became increasingly rarely shot in London – and has never actually been shot in Peckham. It used to be filmed in and around the capital until it became too popular on-screen and the crowds who gathered to watch filming grew too large. 'Filming in London was a pain in the neck and we used to lose a lot of filming time,' says Ray Butt, the show's first producer. 'I remember filming in Chapel Street in London and the crowds used to come round and they wouldn't be quiet and usually we'd have to stop during school breaks. It just became impossible to work.'

'During the early part of the eighties filming in London was always difficult,' agrees Gareth Gwenlan, who produced many of the later episodes. 'One by one, the markets became impossible to use and didn't want to know because filming was too disruptive for them. It also became increasingly

Above: The Trotter gang – Del Boy, Rodney and Grandad.

Right: Whitemead House, in Bristol, plays Nelson Mandela House in Peckham.

Opposite page: Davis Jason and Nicholas Lyndhurst enjoy a laugh on set.

impossible to film with David and Nick on the streets because they would just get mobbed.'

The series was filmed all round the country, and there has been a Nag's Head in Hull, Ipswich, Brighton, London and Bristol and a Peckham street market in Hull, Ipswich, Bristol, and Salisbury. As Ray Butt says: 'You can set up a street market anywhere. All you need is a long run of walls and then put some stalls out.'

Bristol, though, became the most regularly used setting for the show, which ended in 1997. 'Architecturally it had everything we needed in terms of pubs, houses and a market, and most importantly we found the right block of flats,' says Gareth Gwenlan. So instead of Harlech Tower, Park Road East, Acton, London – the original setting – Whitemead House, in Duckmore Road, Bristol became Nelson Mandela House for the duration of filming, and residents got used to seeing Del's dodgy yellow three-wheeler parked nearby.

The Benbom Brothers funfair at Margate was used for the episode 'The Jolly Boys' Outing', as was the Roman Galley pub in Thanet Way, Canterbury and the forecourt of Margate railway station.

The hilarious scene when Raquel gave birth to Damian Trotter was supposed to be in Peckham, but was actually filmed at the maternity wing of Hillingdon Hospital in Uxbridge in the episode 'Three Men, A Woman and a Baby'. The scenes of his christening in 'Miami Twice: The American Dream' were actually filmed at two different churches. The interior scenes were filmed at St John's Church in Ladbroke Grove, London and the outside shots were done at St John's Church in Kentish Town, London.

The Nag's Head used for the 1992 Christmas Special 'Mother Nature's Son' was the White Admiral Pub at Lower Bevendean in Brighton, not far from the allotments in Natal Road which were used as Granddad's old allotment in Peckham.

The Batman and Robin scene in 'Heroes and Villains' was filmed at a Bristol shopping precinct and when the Trotters finally became millionaires in the last episode 'Time On Our Hands', the auction scenes were filmed at Sotheby's, 34-35 New Bond Street, London.

TO THE MANOR BORN

Cricket St Thomas, Chard, Somerset

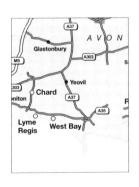

The BBC had a winner on its hands in 1979 with its comedy series *To The Manor Born*. The show starred Penelope Keith as frightfully posh Audrey Fforbes-Hamilton who, stung by death duties, was forced to sell her stately home, Grantleigh Manor, and live in the estate's tiny lodge, taking her butler Brabinger and her beagle, Benjie, with her.

Grantleigh Manor was bought by self-made millionaire grocer Richard De Vere who, certainly in the

Above: Cricket House was the fictional stately home of Richard De Vere in *To The Manor Born.*

eyes of Mrs Fforbes-Hamilton, didn't come from the right kind of background to live in a such a place.

The series was filmed on the elegant Cricket St Thomas estate, near Chard in Somerset. Cricket House naturally played Grantleigh Manor, and the estate's lodge played Mrs Fforbes-Hamilton' modest residence.

The estate was bought in 1998 by Warner Holidays and the house, which was built in 1785 and is Grade II listed, has been turned into a luxury resort hotel offering four-star accommodation and a choice of restaurants.

The rest of the 1,000-acre estate is taken up by a wildlife park which conserves endangered species from around the world in a naturalistic environment, and it also takes part in international breeding programmes.

To The Manor Born was written by Peter Spence, who lived near Cricket St Thomas and who is married to Jill, sister of the estate's former owner John Taylor. 'Obviously when he'd written it he realised he was writing about some of the things that went on here, tongue in cheek,' says John Taylor. 'There were one or two truisms!'

There were some real-life similarities between *To The Manor Born* and John's ownership of the estate. For example, both John and Richard De Vere bought their estates after the previous owner died, and like Richard De Vere, John's mother lived at the house.

To The Manor Born is still responsible for bringing thousands of visitors to Cricket St Thomas Wildlife Park each year, and its international popularity has helped to bring visitors from as far afield as America and Sweden. When Cricket St Thomas Wildlife Park was first opened to the public in 1967 it was solely a wildlife park, but has since had many other attractions. In addition to the animals, which include leopards, lynx, jaguars and sea lions, there are woodland walks, a children's pets corner and a scenic railway. Surrounding the house itself are 16 acres of beautiful gardens including a large Atlas Cedar tree, in the shade of which, it is said, once stood a seat on which Admiral Nelson and Lady Hamilton spent many an hour.

The Cricket St Thomas Wildlife Park is open to the public throughout the year. Telephone (01460) 30111 for further details. For details of how to book accommodation at Cricket St Thomas telephone Warner Holidays on (0870) 6016012.

PERSUASION

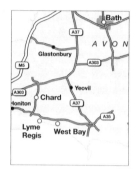

The 1995 version of *Persuasion* was arguably the BBC's finest adaptation of a Jane Austen novel by virtue of Director Roger Michell's deliberately dowdily realistic costumes and settings, making it altogether less glossy than other Austen dramatisations.

Set in 1813, *Persuasion*, Austen's first novel, tells the story of 29-year-old Anne Elliot who lives at Kellynch Hall with her spendthrift father Sir Walter Elliot and elder sister Elizabeth. Eight-and-a-half years previously, Anne had been persuaded to refuse an offer of marriage from a man she loved. He was then a young naval officer with little money and no standing. Now back from the Napoleonic Wars Captain Wentworth has both wealth and position. They meet again, but Anne can only dream of what might have been as he courts her brother's sister-in-law Louisa. Anne receives the determined attentions of her cousin William, but her heart still lies with handsome Captain Wentworth. Both need to persuade each other that their original feelings still remain.

Much of the BBC's adaptation, which starred Amanda Root as Anne, Ciarán Hinds as Captain Wentworth and Corin Redgrave as Sir Walter, was filmed in Bath, with both the Assembly Rooms and the Pump Room being used for some scenes, including a concert.

The nearby Abbey Churchyard also featured, as did 13 Old Bond Street, now a Starbucks coffee shop, which coincidentally played a teashop. A private house at 94 Sydney Place was used as several different screen settings.

Outside Bath, beautiful Sheldon Manor at Chippenham, the surviving manor house of a long gone mediaeval village, doubled as The Musgroves' home. However, it is not currently open to the public.

Barnsley House at Barnsley near Cirencester in Gloucestershire played Kellynch Hall in *Persuasion* and although the house is not open to the public, its beautiful gardens are. For details telephone (01285) 740281.

The famous cob at Lyme Regis, also used for the filming of the movie *The French Lieutenant's Woman*, which starred Meryl Streep and Jeremy Irons and was shot all round the town, was also used for the key moment when Louisa was injured.

POLDARK

Bottallack Manor, Cornwall

Cornwall was the setting for *Poldark*, the BBC's swashbuckling saga about heroic war veteran Ross Poldark, played by Robin Ellis. Set in the 18th century, and based on the novels by Winston Graham, the series was a huge hit with viewers both in Britain and around the world, who revelled in the stories of tin mining, smuggling and skulduggery.

Ross and his wife Demelza, played by Angharad Rees, live at Nampara, which is actually a delightful stone farmhouse, Botallack Manor, built in 1665. Scenes were filmed inside the farmhouse in the dining room, the breakfast room and in one of the bedrooms, and the front lawn outside was used for a memorable scene when Ross Poldark was arrested by redcoats for alleged wrecking. 'It was fantastic,' owner Joyce Cargeeg recalls. 'They were all on horses and they dragged Ross off to prison.'

Before shooting began outside, the production team made sure they removed all signs of 20th century life like outside lights, modern door handles and gates. Since *Poldark*, Botallack Manor has made another appearance on television as Roslyn House in the BBC series *Penmarric*.

The farmhouse is now open to bed and breakfast guests and fans of the series often come to stay from places as far afield as Iceland, Africa and the Caribbean. '*Poldark* has been very good for business,' says Joyce. She can be contacted for details at Botallack Manor Farm, Botallack, Near St Just, Cornwall or by telephone on (01736) 788525. Other scenes at Nampara were filmed at nearby Pendeen Manor.

Ross' cousin Francis Poldark, played by Clive Francis, and his wife Elizabeth, the woman Ross had always wanted to marry, lived at Trenwith. In the first series Trenwith was played by Tudor Godolphin House at Godolphin Cross. Godolphin House was used when Trenwith was sacked and burnt. For the famous fire scene, BBC technicians re-created part of the house in the courtyard and then burnt the set down. Godolphin was also featured in scenes when Trenwith was attacked by miners, and the scenes at the Redruth Fair where Ross Poldark first met Demelza were also shot in the grounds.

Godolphin House is open to the public at certain times of the year and attracts many visitors from overseas. It is open on Thursday afternoons in May and June from 2-5pm; on Tuesday and Thursday afternoons from 2-5pm in July and September; on Tuesdays 2-5pm and on Thursday from 10am-1pm and from 2-5pm in August; and at other times during the year for parties by arrangement. Further details are available from owner Mrs Mary Schofield on (01736) 762409. *Poldark* writer Winston Graham actually based Trenwith on Trerice, a National Trust house near Newquay, which was also used for the film *Twelfth Night*. For details on Trerice telephone: (01637) 875404.

In later episodes a house on the private Boconnoc

Estate near Lostwithiel was used as Trenwith but it is not open to the public nor is it visible from the road.

Doctor Dwight Enys' home in the series is actually Doyden Castle, a gothic folly built by an ex-governor of Wandsworth Prison in the 19th century. The folly, at Port Quin in north Cornwall, is high up on the cliffs and has spectacular views of the sea. The folly can actually be hired from the National Trust on a self-catering basis, but book early as there is usually a very long waiting list.

Port Quin was also the scene of the wrecking of a ship, in which Poldark's arch-rivals, the Warleggan family, had shares. Dozens of locals were recruited as extras to play hungry wreckers and were addressed by the director with a megaphone. Barrels, wood and sacks were placed in the sea by BBC props people and at the appointed time everyone rushed into the sea and collected what spoils they could.

Poldark star Robin Ellis, writing in his 1978 book *Making Poldark*, recalls how seriously some people took the scene: 'Truly there was a wrecking going on. The fighting over the spoils looked so real, I swear a lot of private scores were settled in the sea that morning. I heard one of the professional stuntmen working with us shouting desperately to a very excited Cornishman, "Here, hold on mate – it's only a play."

'It took at least three shouts of "Cut" through the megaphone before order was restored enough for the director to announce that he wanted to do it all over again. And do you know, everyone was delighted.'

The history of Port Quin itself is interesting. The

village was deserted after most of the menfolk were killed by a storm while at sea during the last century. The National Trust has now restored the stone fishing cottages and they are rented out as holiday homes.

Not far from Port Quin, at Trebetherick, is 700-year-old St Enodoc Church which was used for the wedding of Francis and Elizabeth. Another church, Towednack, was used for Francis' father's funeral.

Lots of filming took place on the north coast from Botallack in the far west to the River Camel where Padstow stands, in the Penzance area and on the south coast at Charlestown, which was also used for the 1998 ITV drama *Frenchman's Creek*, and Prussia Cove.

Cornwall doubled as France in the second series with part of the Fowey Estuary, near Lerryn Creek playing a landing point for Ross and his friends in their bid to free Doctor Enys from a French prison, Fort Baton, which was, in fact, St Mawes Castle at the entrance to Falmouth Castle. St Mawes Castle is an English Heritage property and is open to the public.

The interior shots of the tin mine seen in the series was a mock-up in a BBC studio but you can see a real mine, called the Poldark Mine, at Wendron. The mine is now a major tourist attraction and includes a *Poldark* exhibition and many other features. For further details telephone (01326) 563166. For more details on Cornwall contact the tourist board on (01872) 274057.

THE ONEDIN LINE

Dartmouth, Devon

Anyone who visited Dartmouth in Devon during certain periods of the 1970s must have thought they had walked through a time tunnel. For the clock was turned back on much of the town and surrounding areas while the BBC filmed its popular period drama *The Onedin Line.*

The drama, which was set in the 1860s, followed the life of James Onedin, played by Peter Gilmore with side-whiskers, as he ran his shipping line. Originally Liverpool was to have been used to film the series, but the BBC turned to the West Country because they wanted to use the Devon-based three-masted schooner *The Charlotte Rhodes* as their main sailing ship.

In a 1971 booklet on the programme, Producer Peter Graham Scott explained why he chose Dartmouth to play 19th century Liverpool. 'Architecturally the town had much to offer,' he wrote, 'with an authentic Victorian quay at Bayard's Cove, a functional Market Square, another fine quay at Kingsweir, and many narrow streets, alleys and warehouses.'

Bayard's Cove, which hasn't really changed at all since filming, includes the old Customs House and The Dartmouth Arms which was featured in several episodes.

During filming in Bayard's Cove, street lights were changed to old-fashioned gas-lights, No Parking signs and TV aerials were removed, and sawdust and straw were used to cover up modern road markings.

Scenes set in foreign countries were very common in the series – but in reality they were always filmed just round the corner. Bayard's Cove Fort, which was built in 1509, was used as an Arabian market scene, the outside of the George and Dragon in Clarence Street played in another Arabian episode and a Chinese scene was filmed in Avenue Gardens.

Across the River Dart, the quay at Kingsweir doubled as Wilmington in the United States and the Maltster's Arms, formerly owned by television chef Keith Floyd and then known as Floyd's Inn (Sometimes), at Tuckenhay was used as a sailmaker's yard in Australia. Also in Tuckenhay is the old paper mill which was used for a fire sequence. The mill still stands but has now been converted into holiday homes.

The River Dart itself was even used to play the upper reaches of the River Amazon when the crew of the *Charlotte Rhodes* were seen heading up it in canoes. Other locations in Dartmouth that were also used for filming include St Saviour's Church, where James and Anne were married, the historic market place and the Dartmouth Pottery which became a chandlery and a toffee shop.

Outside Dartmouth, the basin at Exeter was used frequently for scenes involving ships unloading by big warehouses, but the new M5 motorway in the mid 1970s brought use of the location to a halt. The M5 bridge over the River Exe was too low for the tall ships used for the series.

The late Geraint Morris, who produced some of the later series of *The Onedin Line*, recalled: 'Because of the expense and time of unstepping the masts when I took over, I was strongly advised to look for another location.' He found his new location at Milford Haven in Wales which fitted the bill perfectly because of its closed dock, and the inlets further up the estuary in deep water were ideal doubles for various foreign scenes. Resourceful as ever, the BBC filmed storm sequences at Milford Haven by tying ropes to the top of the masts and rocking the boat back and forth. They also got the local fire service to spray water over the top and successfully convinced viewers they were in the middle of a tropical storm.

The docks at Gloucester were also used and because the quayside is relatively low the *Charlotte Rhodes* looked quite big. Said Geraint Morris: 'If we'd gone to Liverpool, the drop between quayside and the water level is so large that our ships would have looked like rowing boats.' In later series Falmouth in Cornwall was used for filming. Said Geraint: 'And we continued to go all around the world without being more than four miles off-shore!'

THE CAMOMILE LAWN

Broom Park, Veryan, Cornwall

Fans of the 1992 Channel Four drama *The Camomile Lawn* will be delighted to know that they can actually stay at the attractive Edwardian cliff-top house used in the series. Keith and Lindsay Righton, who live there with their two children, run it as a bed and breakfast hotel. When filming took place in 1991 Lindsay and Keith had already planned to open the house up to bed and breakfast visitors. 'We had decided to do the B&B before *The Camomile Lawn* was filmed, but by the time they had finished filming it was July and it wasn't really worth starting doing anything,' says Lindsay. 'So we didn't actually start doing the B&B until Easter 1992.'

By then *The Camomile Lawn* had been on television, and newspapers had written about the house. The publicity helped the Rightons to start their business. 'The timing couldn't have been better,' says Lindsay.

Many of the people who stayed at the house during 1992 did so because they'd seen it on television, but recently trade has mainly consisted of people who have had the house recommended to them. And Lindsay thinks that's down to good service rather than *The Camomile Lawn*.

Very little had to be done to the outside of the house before filming of *The Camomile Lawn* began, but the interior had to be redecorated three times to reflect the different periods in the drama. Every time this happened the family had to move lock, stock and barrel up to the former servants' quarters on the top floor. But after filming ended, Channel Four redecorated the house to their taste.

The house, which was built in 1908 and is actually owned by the National Trust, has wonderful views of the sea, but Lindsay says it might not be everyone's ideal home when it gets stormy in the winter. 'We're very happy here, although other people may not wish to live right on the edge of a cliff in the teeth of a gale, and the upkeep of the house is quite substantial. It's very exposed, so if the wind

blows the central heating bill goes through the roof!'

If you fancy spending a holiday there call Lindsay or Keith on (01872) 501803 or fax them on (01872) 501109. Lindsay also runs a catering business with her partner Jenny Parnwell and the pair of them did the catering for the funeral scene in *The Camomile Lawn*. Jenny in turn runs a B&B at Lanherriot Farm in the beautiful nearby town in Fowey, which was used by the BBC for the film *The Lord of Misrule*. For details on Lanherriot Farm telephone (01726) 832637 or check out the website on http://www.saqnet.co.uk/users/hanherriot

Below: Beautiful cliff side views at Veryan, Cornwall – you can see Broom Park in the distance, which featured in *The Camomile Lawn*.

Inset: Inside Broom Park.

CASUALTY

Brunel College of Arts and Technology, Ashley Down, Bristol

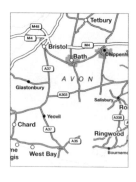

Back in 1985 when members of a BBC production team were hunting for a location to play a fictitious inner-city hospital in a new hard-hitting medical drama called *Casualty* they soon came to one major conclusion: a real-life hospital was out of the question. That decision was reached after they had visited every hospital in Bristol, where the series was to be made, and decided that trying to film a television series at a real-life working hospital was just not practical.

Even though they only wanted the location for exterior shots, because the interior scenes were to be filmed at a specially built hospital set on an industrial estate in another part of the city, the thought of camera teams and actors getting in the way of real ambulance crews ferrying real casualties into hospital was a major fear. 'None of the hospitals we looked at fitted the bill as access to them would have been very difficult because they were proper working hospitals,' explained *Casualty* founder Producer the late Geraint Morris, who also produced other hit shows like *The Onedin Line* and *Wycliffe*, and who sadly died in 1997. 'Then one of the production team said to me: "I've passed an old orphanage that looks a bit like a hospital, is it worth going to see?" I said: "Let's give it try," so we went and had a look and when we got there I said: "This is it!'"

The site had not been used as an orphanage for many years and had become home to the Brunel College of Arts and Technology. The old grey stone buildings certainly looked the part of an old style hospital, and fortunately the college authorities agreed to let the BBC use the site for filming. Picking Brunel College has proved to be a wise choice because the college has been a perfect location for the series. 'The college authorities have been wonderful in allowing us to be there for the last eight years,' said Geraint. 'I can't speak too highly of them. We've been there during term-time and at night and although we're conscious that we are intruding on their activities, they've always been good and we do our best not to shoot at inconvenient times. We liaise closely with the college and try and arrange filming so that it is out of term-time.'

Before filming began, the production team built the now familiar Accident and Emergency awning onto the side of a building in the college's construction department and put in crash barriers on the grass area which is used as a turning circle for vehicles. The crash barriers are covered up or taken down when filming isn't taking place. The BBC also painted a yellow box junction beside the awning and Holby City Hospital signs are put up to cover up the college's signs. The signs make the college look so much like a real hospital that people have come into the grounds to see if it is a new NHS facility. And when *Casualty* finally ends, the BBC has agreed in its contract with the college to take the awning down, remove

Brunel College, where *Casualty* is filmed.

Inset: The false Accident and Emergency entrance at Brunel College of Arts.

the crash barriers and generally put everything back as it was before they arrived.

In addition to the main Accident and Emergency entrance and the ambulance parking area, various other parts of the college have also been used in various episodes including corridors and even the Principal's Office.

Hundreds of other locations around Bristol have been used for *Casualty* over the years, and the show's two location managers are always seeking new ones. In fact, a few years ago they even advertised in the local paper, the *Bristol Evening Post*, for people to send in details of their properties if they thought they might be suitable for the series. 'We are forever looking for new locations and we got a very good reaction,' said Geraint.

The crew also travelled to Southampton in the spring of 1998 to film the wedding of Charlie and Baz on the ship *SS Shieldhall* – which is moored at Ocean Village, Southampton – and to Portsmouth, where a major shopping centre explosion sequence was shot at the eyesore Tricorn Centre, itself due for real demolition in 1999.

In January 1999, the BBC began a new spin-off series *Holby City*, which shows what happens in the rest of Holby City Hospital and features a whole new team of medics along with brief appearances by the *Casualty* team. *Holby City* isn't filmed in Bristol, and interiors are actually shot on a formerly empty floor of a tower block at Elstree Studies in Hertfordshire, near where the BBC also films *EastEnders*. Like the set for *The Bill*, the *Holby City* wards and offices look real, with little signs of them being a film set.

THE HOUSE OF ELIOTT

Bristol

Modern-day Bristol played 1920s London for the BBC's multi-million pound period drama *The House of Eliott*. The city was chosen to double as the capital because it is far easier and cheaper to film outside London, and the houses in parts of Bristol are similar to those in the part of London in which the series is set.

The exterior of Beatrice and Evangeline's House of Eliott design studio was filmed at number 24 Berkeley Square. The Square was selected for the series because the Edwardian and Georgian buildings are very similar to those in a typical London square and many of them are listed, so very few of their original features have been changed. It is also perfect because most of the buildings in the square are business premises which were closed on Sundays when much of the filming took place. When the BBC arrived, they had to remove all traces of the 1990s to re-create London of the 1920s.

Yellow lines were covered up with either latex paint or special mats which looked like cobblestones, and the top of parking meters were removed and covers were put over the posts to make them look like 1920s bollards. The tops of modern streetlights were also removed and replaced with 1920s versions, and where modern venetian blinds or fluorescent lights could be seen they were covered up. Modern intercom systems on the outside of many of the buildings were always a problem and were usually disguised as old-fashioned doorplates.

The Bristol branch of Coutts, in Corn Street, was used to play the fictional Gillespie Saroyan Bank and Clifton Girls School played home to Jack's apartment. The Wills Memorial Building at Bristol University, which has a high tower, also played the interior of the Houses of Parliament and the former Will's Cigarette Factory was used as Jack's film studio.

Royal Fort House, in Royal Fort Gardens, played the offices of a rival fashion house, Hauseurs, and the road outside was converted into a cobbled street using a 'carpet' of rubber cobbles. Clifton Hill House, one of the University's halls of residence, was used for a dinner party scene and the Orangery at another hall of residence, Goldney House, doubled as a teashop.

Just across the River Avon at Leigh Woods is Leigh Court, a former mental hospital, which was used on the programme to play the interior of the Houses of Parliament, the interior of Buckingham Palace and the foyer of the Ritz Hotel.

The impressive Pump Room in Cheltenham was used for several fashion shows, and the bandstand outside was used, not surprisingly, as a bandstand. The Assembly Rooms in Bath have been used, first as an auction room, and later for a charity ball: the Guildhall was used for a charity concert; and the City's Royal Victoria Park doubled as Hyde Park.

HARBOUR LIGHTS

West Bay, Dorset

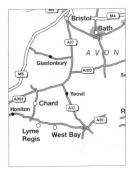

At the beginning of 1999, the villagers of the small Dorset village of West Bay, just two miles from its larger neighbour Bridport, were bracing themselves for an influx of visitors anxious to catch a glimpse of the real-life setting for the BBC1 drama *Harbour Lights*.

Judging by the popularity of his last major series *Heartbeat*, Nick Berry was the obvious choice to play a harbour master, ex-Royal Navy Lieutenant Commander Mike Nicholls. He is in charge of the harbour of a small south coast town where feuding families, ruthless business dealings and the sea dominate the lives of the people who work and play there. Life is never quiet in Bridehaven.

Nick Berry is joined in the cast by former *Coronation Street* star Tina Hobley, who plays WPC Melanie Rush, whose dealings with the harbour master could be more than just professional, and Matilda Zieger as Jane Ford, the sister of a navy diver who died under Mike's command.

'Being a harbour master is an important job,' Nick explains. 'He's employed by the local council and he's in charge of the harbour and also the coast for about a ten- mile radius.' For filming he gets to drive a powerful rigid inflatable boat, and he fell in love with the machine. 'It's great fun and the best bit,' he smiles. 'It was easy to learn how to drive. It's

Nick Berry and Louis Mahoney on location for *Harbour Lights*.

Inset: The door to Nick Berry's flat in *Harbour Lights* – formerly a toilet!

absolutely boys and toys stuff. One day we were out at sea on a boat and all these dolphins swam over and were darting about alongside us,' he recalls. 'That was just the most amazing thing I've ever seen like that in this country. It was unbelievable. It was like they knew the cameras were there and were able to film them, and we've used some of the footage on the opening title sequence for the programme.'

The quaint real-life 16th century Bridport Arms Hotel, close to the sea, is one of the show's key locations and actually plays two different places in the series. The end nearest the sea plays the Pier Hotel and the other end doubles as The Bridehaven. One of the bedrooms plays the Pier Hotel's landlady's room, and the pub's television lounge was turned half into a kitchen complete with equipment. 'We just didn't use them at all while they were filming,' says landlord John Jacobs, who has run the pub with his wife Carla since 1985. 'It looked very different. It was full of commercial kitchen appliances, none of them connected, of course, and they painted the wall by the range brown to make it look well used. Afterwards they put it back how we wanted, which included leaving the swing doors they'd put in place.'

The pub is a historic building, the oldest in West Bay, and was originally a farm. One part contained a small fisherman's bar. The section of the pub where the restaurant now stands used to be the farmyard. Inevitably for a building of its age there have been reports that the pub is haunted. 'I'm personally a bit of a sceptic,' says John Jacobs. 'But people have reported seeing the ghost of an old fisherman.'

Ghosts aside, John is sure the series will be good news for

his trade. 'I'd be very surprised if the series wasn't good for business,' he says. 'We were very pleased to have the BBC film unit here. They were a very nice crowd and didn't create any problems. They did their very best to keep disruption to a minimum. The cast and crew were very nice and Nick Berry is smashing. He's just like he seems to be on TV, he's very friendly and down-to-earth.'

The Bridport Arms Hotel offers reasonably priced accommodation all year starting at around £23 per person per night for bed and breakfast. For further details telephone: (01308) 422994.

Outside the pub, just to the left, is John Jacobs' bottle store, formerly a public toilet (not that it looks much like that now). When the BBC arrived they removed the bricks from the bricked-up windows, put in new frames, built a false porch on the front and changed the door. It now looks just like a cottage and plays the entrance to Mike Nicholls' fictional home. The door opens but only leads into a small hallway. The interior to the cottage is actually filmed elsewhere in a flat in the village.

Just a stone's throw from the Bridport Arms is the Harbour Café which plays an integral part of life in Bridehaven. On-screen it is run by music-loving Elvis, who is played by actor Louis Mahoney, whereas off-screen it is owned by husband and wife Ray and Carole Bowell. 'We closed the café while the BBC were filming in it,' explains Carole. 'Which was wonderful for us because it meant we could have days off in summer for the first time in five years.' Now Carole is hoping that the show will bring an influx of visitors to West Bay, particularly out of season.

Fans of the shows will be delighted to learn that the interior of the café looks almost identical to how it does on-screen because Ray and Carole have let the BBC leave their props in place, making it easier for them to film a second series. The curtains and panelling inside and the canopies outside the café were added by the BBC's design team, and all the posters and the jukebox inside are props along with a mural depicting Elvis' favourite artists. 'If people do come to West Bay after seeing *Harbour Lights* then I think they'd expect to find the café looking the same,' says Carole. The open and closed sign on the café's door is also a reminder of the show. One side reads 'Open' but on the other side it says: 'Elvis has left the building'. 'When the BBC told us that the character running the café was going to be called Elvis we thought it was a wind-up because Ray is a great fan of Elvis Presley,' says Carole.

The on-screen harbour master's office is on the other side of the harbour and the exterior used for filming is the real harbour master's office, although interior scenes are sometimes shot elsewhere to avoid disrupting the work of the real harbour master.

Among the other locations in West Bay that feature in the series is a shop next to the amusement arcade, where the BBC built a fake bingo hall, and the Golf Club, where a fake cemetery was constructed for one episode, as well as several local shops.

Other villages nearby that also appear in the series include Abbotsbury, Symondsbury, Ashley Chase, Seaton and Charmouth.

GRACE AND FAVOUR

Chavenage House, near Tetbury, Gloucestershire

The follow-up series to the classic BBC comedy *Are You Being Served?* was set at a country hotel left to the Grace Brothers staff by old Mr Grace. The exterior shots of the hotel, Millstone Manor, were filmed at privately-owned Chavenage House, at Tetbury, near Stroud, Gloucestershire, a 16th century manor house.

The house, a family home, which isn't far from Prince Charles' home, Highgrove, is open to the public and the owners gladly welcome visitors. It is a beautiful Elizabethan house with an interesting history. For example, during the English Civil War it was owned by Colonel Nathaniel Stephens, who was persuaded by Oliver Cromwell, a relation by marriage, to vote for the King's impeachment. Not long after the King was beheaded, the Colonel died and legend has it that his ghostly form was seen being driven away from Chavenage by a headless coachman wearing Royal vestments.

The BBC did little to the house before the filming of *Grace and Favour* began but did have to alter the adjoining farm, which is part of the Chavenage estate. 'We made the farm more old-fashioned and run down,' says *Grace And*

Favour Production Designer Richard Dupré, 'and added lots of animals and straw. Most of the things you saw in the yard were hired props.' In fact, the chickens seen on screen in *Grace and Favour* are rented for £1 a day from a props firm.

The farm's existing cow sheds needed revamping because they were disused. 'We installed cow stalls and added lots of props like pails and stools to make it look well used,' says Richard. Straw was used extensively round the farm and was given by the estate's owners David and Rona Lowsley-Williams.

An old barn on the estate was perfectly suited to the role of a ramshackle barn in an episode where the Grace Brothers crew found a vintage car, and when the production team needed a pub for a scene they found a perfect example in The Vine Tree in Norton, a village not too far from the location. It was used in the show for exterior shots and Richard and his team didn't even change the name. He says: 'We just left it as it was because it was just right.'

Grace and Favour isn't the only series to have been filmed at Chavenage. It's also been used for episodes of *Poirot, The House of Eliott, Berkeley Square* and *Cider With Rosie.* Chavenage is open to the public for tours every Thursday and Sunday, May to September from 2pm to 5pm, and on Bank Holidays. Visits by parties of more than twenty can be arranged at other times. The house can also be booked for wedding receptions, dinners and conferences. For further details about Chavenage contact Mr David Lowsley-Williams on (01666) 502329.

CALL RED

Portsmouth, Hampshire

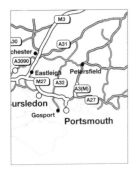

Portsmouth and its surrounding areas were the main settings for the 1996 series *Call Red*, an ITV drama about the crew of an air ambulance. The helipad was supposedly on top of the fictitious King Alfred's Hospital but it was actually built on top of sprawling Fort Widley, which overlooks the city and was built in the 1880s to defend the port in the event of an invasion by the French.

One of the biggest headaches for the production team was building the helideck on which to land the specially adapted Dauphin helicopter, because not only did it need to be a film set but it also needed to be a fully working helipad, built to Civil Aircraft Authority regulations. The noise created by the helicopter angered a few locals, which was strange for a naval port, well used to the noise of military aircraft.

The helipad and operations room cost £125,000 to build and took 25 men two weeks to construct using 220 tonnes of steel, 20 tonnes of timber and hundreds of litres of non-slip MOD grey paint. The lift doors from the helipad actually went nowhere as the hospital interior scenes were filmed in a disused wing at Knowle psychiatric hospital, near Fareham, a few miles away.

The set was then equipped with state-of-the-art medical technology leased from companies all over the world – ironically some of it was not even in use in the NHS at the time of filming. Other scenes for the show, which crashed after just one series, were shot at sea just off Eastney beach, Portsmouth, on ex-navy submarines at Pound's Scrapyard, Portsmouth and at the Camber, Old Portsmouth.

THE BRITTAS EMPIRE

Ringwood Rec. Centre, Parsonage Barn Lane, Ringwood, Hampshire

The BBC comedy about the exploits of Whitbury Leisure Centre manager Gordon Brittas, played by Chris Barrie, was filmed at Ringwood Recreation Centre at Ringwood in Hampshire. The centre continued to be open to the public even when the series was being filmed. 'We'd book the sports hall for a day just like anyone else would,' explains Producer Mike Stephens. 'And the same with the pool and the rest of it.'

The location was picked for two reasons, as Mike Stephens explains: 'Basically I wanted somewhere that looked different, and it has certainly got a different style to it; and also Chris was appearing in a play at Winchester while we were filming so we needed to find somewhere that he could get to easily each day.'

Some leisure centre bosses have failed to see the funny side of *The Brittas Empire* and have written to Mike to complain about the way managers are portrayed. Mike reveals: 'We have had letters in from leisure centre managers saying that it was disgusting that we were taking the mickey out of people who work in leisure centres and asking us why we didn't take the mickey out of the public instead.'

Mike wrote back telling them that they shouldn't take it so seriously. 'And if they do then I think there's something wrong, because it was so outrageous,' he says.

HOWARD'S WAY

Bursledon, Hampshire

The BBC's eighties sex-and-sailing soap *Howard's Way* brought tourists flocking to south Hampshire where the series was filmed.

It was set around the fictional village of Tarrant, played in real life by pretty Bursledon near Southampton. The series focused on the Mermaid Boatyard, owned by Tom Howard and Jack Rolfe, and that was played by the Elephant Boatyard in Land's End Road, but it doesn't welcome sightseers.

However, you can enjoy a quiet drink at the main pub used in *Howard's Way*, The Jolly Sailor just along the road. Halfway down Kew Road is Bondfield House, a private house which played the Howard family home in the series, and just off Kew Lane is Hungerford where Hunt's Folly played the home of Jan's mother Kate Harvey.

The other major location in Hamble is St Leonard's Church in Church Lane which was used for the filming of Lynne Howard and Claude Dupont's wedding.

The BBC was very resourceful in its use of locations to save money, for example, the Victoria Rampart Jetty at nearby Warsash doubled as New York harbour when Lynne Howard crossed the Atlantic single-handedly; the High Street at Hamble played Italy in one episode; and Waddesdon Manor, a National Trust property near Aylesbury, Buckinghamshire played Charles Frere's French château Auban.

Exterior shots of Victoria Rampart offices were also used as Ken Masters' chandlery and Jan Howard's Boutique, and scenes at Ken's powerboat centre were filmed at a real-life showroom on the A27 at Swanwick.

The business park built by tycoon Charles Frere in the series is actually Arlington Securities' Solent Business Park, just off junction nine of the M27, and the marina that Frere built is actually Hythe Marina, at Hythe, near Southampton.

THE RUTH RENDELL MYSTERIES

Romsey, Hampshire

Most major towns in Hampshire have been used at some point for the filming of the *Ruth Rendell Inspector Wexford Mysteries* which began in the late eighties and remain popular today. The country detective, played by veteran actor George Baker, was based at Kingsmarkham – a fictional place played by the town of Romsey near Southampton.

The side entrance of the town's Magistrates Court doubled as the entrance to the police station with the production team adding just a sign and putting police cars in the car park to make it look like the real thing. The inside of the building was actually used as the police station for many of the early episodes, but because it is a working court, TVS and later Meridian, who made the drama, were only allowed to use it at weekends.

Later, the Court was used at weekends too, so a replica of the inside of the police station was built inside a warehouse at Totton, near Southampton, and the Magistrates Court was then only used for exterior shots.

'The replica was good,' says Production Manager Peter Hider. 'We had all the same signs and desks so viewers couldn't tell the difference between the set and the original.'

Many streets in the centre of Romsey were featured in the stories, and the production team became part of the scenery after a while. Most of the restaurants and cafés were used at some point, along with the Job Centre, Romsey Abbey, the Over-Sixties Club, the Corn Market and Palmerston Square.

Two pubs, the Queen Vic and the King William IVth, played Wexford's locals and the house that played his home is also in the town. One Christmas story was filmed in Romsey during July and bemused shoppers found the whole of the town centre decked out with decorations and saw extras wandering round with Christmas trees and presents.

Outside Romsey, St John's Church at Farleigh Chamberlayne near Braishfield was used for a funeral scene; an Indian restaurant called Kuti's in London Road, Southampton, was used for one episode; Sherfield Parish Hall doubled as a police control centre; and Southampton University was used as Brighton University.

The interior scenes for the story 'Speaker of Mandarin', which were supposed to be at a hotel in China, were actually shot at the Botley Park Hotel in Botley. 'We've been almost everywhere in Hampshire,' says Peter. 'Almost every conceivable place in the county has been used at some time. We don't like to travel crews too far because it costs time and money, so we use locations as close to our base as possible. If we can find something on our doorstep it saves us shooting time.'

Winchester College at Winchester has been used; the

King's Theatre at Southsea played The Fontain Cinema; and The Fuzz and Furkin pub in Albert Road, Southsea, formerly the Southsea police station, is just yards away from the theatre. It played a police station in one episode; and a large family home a few roads away doubled as a London town house.

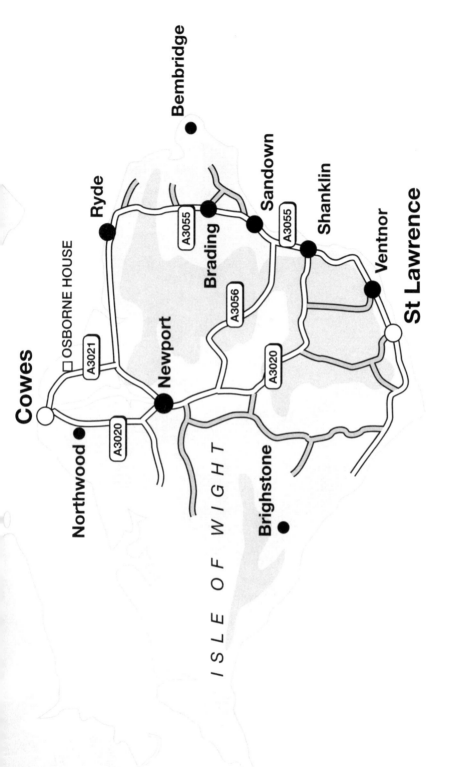

THE ISLE OF WIGHT

MRS BROWN

Osborne House, Isle of Wight

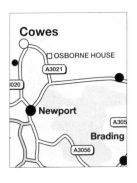

Much of the shooting of the BBC film *Mrs Brown*, which movingly told the poignant and unusual love story between Queen Victoria, played by Judi Dench, and her loyal Highland ghillie John Brown, played by Billy Connolly, took place at Queen Victoria and Prince Albert's real-life retreat, Osborne House on the Isle of Wight.

Victoria married Albert in 1840, three years after she had come to the throne, and they bought the site in 1845 and replaced the existing house with Thomas Cubitt's design for a new home, the building that we see now. It was completed in 1851. The Royal couple found tranquillity at Osborne House with its fine view across the Solent and elegant Italian style away from the formality of Court life at Buckingham Palace and Windsor Castle.

Prince Albert died of typhoid in 1861; the Queen was inconsolable and refused to carry out public duties, even the State Opening of Parliament. Her popularity with the people began to wane and there were calls to abolish the monarchy. As a last resort Sir Henry Posonby, her private secretary, summoned John Brown from Balmoral to walk the Queen's pony, hoping that exercise might encourage her to emerge from her mourning. Brown's arrival began an extraordinary relationship.

A confident Highlander, he had little respect for either the English or Court protocol, and he became the Queen's most trusted companion. 'It's one of the greatest love stories ever told,' says Executive Producer Douglas Rae. 'A love affair that may, or may not, have been physical. But we didn't want to fall into the trap of sensationalising the story. Whatever the truth of that, I think John Brown is probably responsible for us still having a monarchy.'

It was John Brown who drew the Queen back into the world through her love of horses and the outdoors, and it was he who – after persuasion from Prime Minister Disraeli – convinced her to see more of her people. Star Judi Dench, who was nominated for an Oscar for her portrayal of Queen Victoria, is convinced of the depth of Victoria's feeling for John Brown. 'It was true love,' she says. 'After John Brown died, she had a rose laid on his bed every day – and, when she died, she held his photograph in her hand.'

Queen Victoria died on 22 January 1901 on a couch bed in the Queen's Bedroom. The private Royal Suite was closed to all except members of the Royal family until the Queen gave permission for full public access in 1954.

Osborne House is now owned by the English Heritage and is open all year round. For details telephone: (01983) 200022 or the Tourist Information Offices at Cowes (01983) 291914 or Newport (01983) 525450. English Heritage has a website at http://www.english-heritage.org.uk/

LADY CHATTERLEY

Isle of Wight

The Isle of Wight doubled as the South of France for the controversial 1993 BBC production of *Lady Chatterley* which starred Joely Richardson in the title role and Sean Bean as her gamekeeper Mellors.

The Old Park Hotel at St Lawrence (01983) 852583 was the location for the beach and woodland walk scenes and the maze at the clifftop theme park, Blackgang Chine and Lisle Combe, the house at the Rare Breeds and Waterfowl Park at St Lawrence, played Lady Chatterley's father's South of France home, Mandalay.

The house is not generally open to the public but can be seen from the Park and one section of it is open for bed and breakfast. Joely Richardson actually stayed in one of the rooms during a break in filming. For further details telephone Mr and Mrs Noyes on (01983) 852582 or 855144.

Havenstreet Station, part of the Isle of Wight Steam Railway (which runs from Wootton to Smallbrook Junction), was featured in the final episode of the BBC adaptation when Lady Chatterley returns home from France.

The final scene of *Lady Chatterley*, where Mellors and

Connie embrace at the stern of a ship as they set off for Canada, was filmed on the Southampton to Isle of Wight Red Funnel ferry, *Cowes Castle*, which is now no longer in service with the company. The ship doubled as a cross-channel cruise liner sailing from Southampton water. It was picked because it had a traditional wooden handrail and, by cleverly filming from different angles, Director Ken Russell was able to make the ferry look like a liner.

The scenes at Lady Chatterley's home were filmed at Wrotham Park, near Barnet, just north of London, but it is not open to the public.

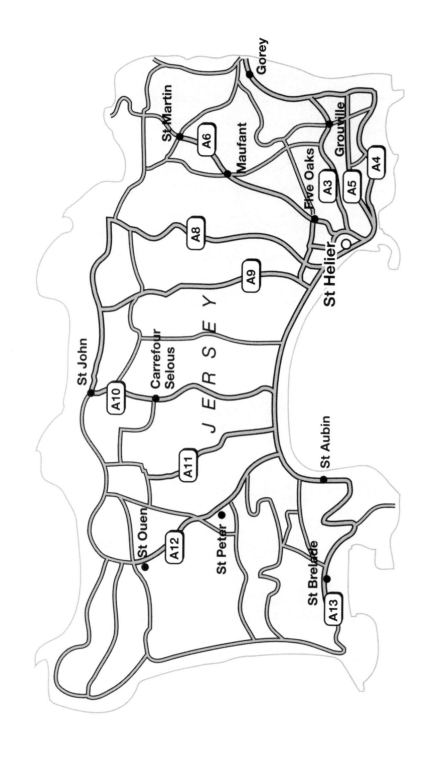

JERSEY

BERGERAC

For an island a mere nine miles long, with a population of just 83,000, there were an awful lot of crimes committed on Jersey during the 1980s – at least on screen. But far from putting visitors off, the success of the BBC detective series *Bergerac* brought visitors flocking to the island. The Jersey tourist authorities were delighted by the publicity, and they even hired the series' star, John Nettles, who played Triumph Roadster-driving Sergeant Jim Bergerac, to appear in their advertisements.

Most of the 45-square-mile island got a look-in at some point during the series' ten-year run, which began in

1981. Lots of the locations used for the series are easy to see, but not even a super-sleuth like Jim Bergerac could find the attractive stone cottage and farm that played his home in many of the early series. It was located in Queen's Valley in the east of the island, and is now under hundreds of thousands of gallons of water as the whole valley was flooded in 1992 to make the new Queen's Valley Reservoir.

Jim's ex-father-in-law, millionaire Charlie Hungerford, who was played by Terrance Alexander, lived in a luxury home, portrayed by two different houses. The first was Noirmont Manor, a beautiful house overlooking Belcroute Bay. In the first episode it was nearly the scene of a disaster when a mechanical digger broke free and fell over the cliff onto the beach below. For a few minutes it was feared that Terrance Alexander, who had been driving it earlier for filming, was in it, but fortunately he wasn't anywhere near. The second house that played Charlie's home was Windward House, which is private, and overlooks St Brelade's Bay.

The Jersey Police Headquarters from which Jim worked, the Bureau des Estrangères (Department for Non -residents), was supposed to be in St Helier but was actually Haute de la Garenne, a former children's home in the Parish of St Martin's in the east of the island, which the BBC also used as a production base during filming. In reality, there is no such police department. The real-life Jersey Police were of great help to the BBC when they filmed *Bergerac*, as John Nettles recalls: 'They were extraordinarily helpful and supportive of what we were trying to do over there and they treated us with kindness and amusement. They also provided us with the materials to make the show – advice about police procedure, the hardware like cars, and all the extras we used for uniformed policemen were real uniformed policemen.'

One of Jim's regular contacts was Diamante Lil, played by actress Mela White, who ran a restaurant and bar called The Royal Barge. In real life the restaurant is The Old Court House at St Aubin, a popular venue for both locals and visitors. Only the exterior was used for filming – the interior of The Royal Barge was a set built inside the old Forum cinema in St Helier.

Around the island dozens of places were used for filming the series. For example, the Round Tower, the most southerly German wartime fortification at Noirmont Point, was used for an action sequence when a stunt man was thrown from the top of the tower to the rocks below after a fight. The Norman Church of St Brelade, which dates back to the 11th century, and its churchyard were used many times for weddings and funerals, and the church hall played the headquarters of a dastardly medium in one episode.

St Ouen's Manor, which dates back to the 13th century, was used repeatedly in the series in various guises as an art gallery and museum, as a French château, as the headquarters of a neo-fascist and as home to an eccentric millionaire, who was robbed by the ice maiden, Philippa Vale, played by Liza Goddard.

Beau Port, an attractive secluded beach, was featured in

an episode where Charlie Hungerford planned to build a huge hotel complex on the valley leading to it and cover the whole bay with a retractable glass dome. Needless to say, like many of Charlie's wilder ideas, it didn't happen, on-or off-screen.

Mount Orgueil Castle was used just once in *Bergerac* in an episode about a German film star, played by Warren Clarke, who was making a movie in Jersey about the German occupation. Jim later had a fight with the character which took place on a large German bunker on the southern headland at St Ouen's Bay. The beach at St Ouen's was featured many times, and in one episode two young surfers found the body of a skin-diver there. Not far away, at St Mary's, on the road from St Ouen to Trinity, is the Ecôlé Elémentairé, which played the school of Jim's daughter Kim.

John Nettles ran into trouble with the real Jersey Police during the filming of one episode when Jim chased a villain across St Brelade's Bay on a jet ski. Afterwards he was ticked off by an angry officer.

Like the viewers, John Nettles fell in love with Jersey while filming *Bergerac*, and he used to have a home there. He has his own idea as to why the series was so popular. 'It was very nice for people in the middle of an English winter to switch on the television and see lovely scenery, sunlit bays and all the rest of those things,' he says. 'And what is nice about Jersey is that, even though it's only nine by five miles, it contains many locations. You might think you are in California if you are down at St Ouen's Beach with the sand dunes behind you, and if you go to the north of the island around Sorel Point you could think that you were in Cornwall, with the grey cliffs, small coves and great beaches. Therefore we could exploit that and we could get a camera crew around very quickly to very different locations. Most people who come across to the island are quite surprised to find out how small it is, because when we were filming we made it look much larger.'

USEFUL FURTHER READING

Bergerac's Jersey by John Nettles **(BBC Books, 1988)**

The Bill – The Inside Story of British Television's Most Successful Police Series by Tony Lynch **(Boxtree, 1991)**

Dad's Army – The Making of a Television Legend by Bill Pertwee **(Pavilion Book, 1998)**

Doctor Who Magazine **(Marvel Comics)**

Doctor Who – The Sixties by David J. Howe, Mark Stammers and Stephen James Walker **(Virgin Publishing, 1992)**

London's Burning – Behind The Scenes With Britain's Favourite Firefighters by Geoff Tibballs **(Boxtree, 1992)**

The Making of *Peak Practice* by Geoff Tibballs **(Boxtree, 1995)**

Making Poldark by Robin Ellis **(Crossaction, 1987)**

The Making of Pride and Prejudice by Sue Birtwistle and Susie Conklin **(Penguin and BBC Books, 1995)**

The Only Fools and Horses Story by Steve Clark **(BBC Books, 1998)**

The World of Inspector Morse by Christopher Bird **(Boxtree, 1998)**

The World of Jonathan Creek by Steve Clark **(BBC Books, 1999)**

Useful Telephone numbers:
English Heritage: 0171 973 3434
The National Trust: 0181 315 1111
The British Tourist Authority: 0181 846 9000

The author would be pleased to receive further location information for possible inclusion in future editions of this book, however he cannot promise to reply to every letter. Details should be sent to: Steve Clark, On Set!, c/o Blake Publishing, 3 Bramber Court, 2 Bramber Road, London, W14 9PB.